EVOLUTION

The Great Deception

Daniel Snuffer

ISBN 978-1-0980-5474-8 (paperback)
ISBN 978-1-0980-5475-5 (digital)

Christian Faith Publishing, Inc.
832 Park Avenue
Meadville, PA 16335
www.christianfaithpublishing.com

Printed in the United States of America

Contents

Chapter 1: Darwinism 5

Chapter 2: Archaeological Forgeries?...........................25

Chapter 3: Lucy...43

Chapter 4: Transitional Fossils?...................................60

Chapter 5: Monkey or Man 72

Chapter 6: Theory or Law 81

Chapter 7: The God with Fifty Names..........................92

Chapter 8: Rock Monkeys 110

Chapter 9: Of Mice and Men 122

Chapter 10: The Ruse..136

Chapter 11: The Bible History of Truth.......................149

Chapter 12: GOD is in His Word..................................158

References 183

Chapter 1

○

Darwinism

Since man took the time to look up into the night sky for the first time, we have wondered about our origins. Five thousand seven hundred and seventy-seven years ago, what would be later known as the Hebrew people began to log their exploits. It would seem that for some people, the mystery of where we came from should have been figured out by now. But you should know, our history is clouded by two conflicting stories. Both stories have been told enough to where we are accustomed to them, but one story is of man; the other, well, you decide.

Our interaction with the world around us leads us to believe that science is the propagator of what we find to be useful and true. If you think this, it is because that is what you have been conditioned to think. Modern Science has been a boon to mankind; some of the most miraculous cures have been made in the twentieth and twenty-first century. But make no mistake, any science must have at its foundation the truth. Any science flawed with anything but the truth is at its foundation flawed. There is a beauty in the truth, and you will know it when you see it, for once you have seen the truth, nothing else makes sense.

These truths are and have had the most prolific impact on the longevity of our species. Any truth is a good one, deceit is not needed, but it is sometimes used by some scientists to get you in their camp. Science is sometimes used as the catch-all phrase to dupe us into believing that they, the educated (evolutionist), possess knowledge that we are barely smart enough to understand. There underline agenda is more than a theory as we will soon find out.

Like anything, even science can either be used for good or not-so-good purposes; evolution is a religion concocted by man and displayed as the alternative to the non-thinking biblical perspective. If you don't think so, try and get tenure in a college of higher learning and proclaim your belief in GOD. If you in any way attack the institution of evolution, you will lose your job and will have difficulty finding another one. This process is termed excommunication, meaning you are lost from the religion of evolutionary science and will not be allowed back until you mend your evil ways. You will need to renounce GOD and his old book of fairy tales as penitence and mend your evil ways.

While the population is roughly 2 percent atheist, when you look at the field of science, 17 percent of scientists proclaim there is no GOD. Therefore, almost one in five scientists thinks you have a mental condition if you believe in GOD. It's okay because they can cure your mental condition with their wisdom. They are committed to enlighten you and want to help. "I am here to enlighten you with my superior point of view." You no longer need the opium of the masses because science is here to save you. Science is the truth, and the truth will set you free. But is evolution really science?

One example is, many atheists claim that your GOD has told you the earth is flat. They expound that if there is a GOD, he is lying to you; and if GOD lies, then there is really no GOD. Some people are intimidated with the miraculous intelligence of our scientist/atheist friends and look no further. The argument is a ridiculous one because it proves nothing but the atheist personal point of view and their interpretation of a line of scripture. After all, by their intelligence alone, they are the judges of the truth even if it is a manipulation of scanty and frail facts. Believing they have worked out the details of their theories, they tough it as if it were the new law.

Defending your point of view is difficult at best, because the atheist will ask some obscure handpicked line of scripture. Answering will require you to read the entire Bible, instantly right now to prove them wrong. This is a trick obviously constructed to get you to shut up so they can take the floor to expand your mind and propagate their disbelief. Their quest is not to enlighten you or even themselves, but for them (the evolutionist), it usually revolves around a brainwashing session where the object is to revisit and reinforce wild speculation with little or no facts. The truth is, simply they are brainwashing themselves by trying to brainwash you.

They are willing and ready to confront you. After all, they have a lot of convincing to do; 2 percent of the population isn't exactly a majority, and time is wasting. The narcissism of the scientist/atheist will not allow any discussion of any truth; they don't provide to the listener now turned into a student. They went to college for ten years and will not listen to some half-baked fairy tales that are from an almost six-thousand-year-old history book.

Years and years on the campus have taught them all they need to know, and they want to teach it to you and, of course, your children. They are ready to puke up their own fairy tales, to beat back the injustice of ambiguity and outright silliness of the Bible. If you think, however, "how dare you" attack the institution of science, you're right, but my problem isn't with 73 percent of the scientists, only that 17 percent. As we will see, evolution is not and cannot be considered a science, for it is only a theory full of holes and wishful thinking.

The oldest ruse in the book is to claim that GOD depicts the earth as flat. Well, does the Bible say the earth is flat? No, the Bible doesn't say that at all. Revelation 7:1 speaks about four angels standing at the four corners of the earth. Most believing people interpret this passage as referring to the four directions—north, south, east, and west. If you over rationalize anything, it leads you to a path where you will have a hard time getting off.

The concept to the Bible reader is a much larger understanding than angels standing on the corners of a square block. The four corners (directions) denote dominion over the four corners of the universe, pretty big, huh? Evolutionist, we get it; your point of view matters a lot to you. The intelligent person has a need and wants their special talent recognized. Who wouldn't? It is a natural desire that we all have. It drives us it makes us strong; it feels pretty darn good, doesn't it? "Tell the truth." The simple reality is that something as simple as a belief system are used to force a round peg into a square hole and by the way, don't bible thumpers look silly?

There is only one problem, over rationalization leads to personal obsession. I think the proper word is vanity. You know, that dirty little six letter word. The one that we would be insulted if some told you, "You're vain!" An atheist view is one of vanity; they must propose an improbable question to get the floor to show you just how smart they really are. As a Christian, we should say, "You've read the Bible?" Most times, they will say yes, which means they want you to believe they read the entire Bible and threw it out, because their superior intelligence has saved them form a life of GOD's old book of fables. But the truth is, they spend a large part of their time trying to convince themselves animal worship is okay. The simple truth is especially if the animals have been dead a long time; those ones are the best rocks also known as fossils. The intent of this book is to give the reader ammunition to combat the most fanatical evolutionary theorist out there. It is a simple debate, is GOD real or is Lucy really the link to a past that cannot be proven?

The real truth is, they may have read the passage somewhere in the Bible, but as far as reading it cover to cover, the truth is really no. If you can close your eyes to the truth, it's easy to understand why others see what the evolutionist sees. I have read the Bible twice; I believed it the first time I read it and also the last. I believe it now! It is a question of disbelief for our scientist/atheist fellows. The truth of the Bible proves itself time and time again. To know the Bible is to know the relevant history of man—past, present, and against all the odds, man's future.

The atheist has closed their heart to a much deeper truth; they, in their disbelief, may never fully comprehend. Why? Well, let's use science to answer the question, probably the science that the 73 percent believe. Out of all the sciences, evolution is definitely the newest or it would be if it were truly a science. It might be new, but they— the evolutionists—are the high priest of the atheist cult. Science is great as long as everyone realizes you should stick to your own field. But evolutionist uses other sciences to try and prove their point of view. It is a nice thought, but sciences that once helped evolution now are providing an evolutionary pause.

This observance is even better realized when the atheist finds out he just doesn't get the science of religion. Sorry, atheist, you get an F in realizing no matter how loud you get, you're in the minority. Your theory is just too hard to believe with little or no evidence. I have heard the slings and arrows, and we are all a little tired of the anti-religion jargon. If it is fair or not to criticize or to be critical of anyone, or to judge and in your imaginations, you pass judgment on the masses that will not buy your half-baked rhetoric. While some may question the reason why the reality is much more profound, it seems some of us have seen through the lie.

This shouldn't be done solely on wild speculation or a hunch attained from staring at fossilized bones for way too long. Some, like the evolution story and pass judgment on others, are based solely on the concept "there is no GOD." Oh, really now? On the subject of GOD, atheist try to go through the believing man as quickly as possible. This is so they are free to target the next knuckle-dragging, Bible thumper they meet. Well, if fair is fair, then if you can dish it out, it's time to see if you can take it.

Neanderthal man, extinct, why? This is a serious question as all of us can agree on. This is because if we can find out why they went extinct, then we have a leg up on their mistakes and possibly avert the disaster for our species. You can read all day on the internet on why and get conjecture half-truths and fantasy. But what makes the most sense is, a species usually goes extinct because of a very simple truth that most of us can totally agree on. What is the answer? Well, losing the ability to reproduce faster than the population dying usually does the trick. Ask the passenger pigeon; it laid only one egg instead of the occasional two like its other pigeon cousins. Extinct!

When it was hunted as a food source, it disappeared in one generation, once numbering in the billions. Overhunting, low population numbers, forced what few were left to reproduce with their cousins, now they are gone forever. Neanderthal, and let's face it, it was a human in every aspect except he had a larger brain than the rest of us. Didn't help him much overall, but the truth is he had habits that made his plight doomed as soon as his habits came in conflict with the reality of his situation.

His ability to maintain genetic diversity was hampered by the trading of women between tribes. Anthropologist knows this, because the study of hunter-gatherers requires them to live and move in small groups. This coupled with the fact that small numbers are easier to sustain. The availability of food enhances survival in smaller groups. Neanderthal could not support a large number of people. Hunter-gatherers almost always have an inconsistent food source, and smaller numbers improve success for the group—"less mouths to feed."

We know this from the science of anthropology, which is a real science. The females were treated pretty badly; their usefulness was mostly to procreate and a few berries freshly picked was a plus, but for the most part, having babies was a woman's main function in life. Genetic necessity required new blood in the gene pool, so women constantly moved from one tribe to another to accommodate the needs of the species. His genetic structure (Neanderthal) is different from ours. Of course, it is, and so some scientists think he is our cousin and not the ancestor some would have you believe.

He was definitely different. The genes prove it. What I have investigated is interesting because when you put the whole story together, what do we have? The facts are clearly laid out and provide the following information:

1. Small groups hunter gatherer. (Fact)
2. Using women as baby machines. (Necessity)
3. Trading for a new woman now and then. (Genetic necessity)
4. Immorality? (Yes, by definition?)
5. Interbreeding? (Very highly probability?)

These are the concepts laid out by science, and I believe in any science that makes sense. Inbreeding for even a short time will cause two things according to real science. A distinct gene pattern will develop, and that pattern will be different than other species with a wider range of genetic influx. Also continued inbreeding causes sterility, deformity, and disease.

Even creatures of the same species will lose the ability to procreate with its own species, if separated long enough from its genetically diverse relatives. In truth, continued inbreeding brings eventual death for any species that breaks this biblical law. In essence, like the passenger pigeon, deaths outnumbered births. The Neanderthal man went extinct, because his evolutionary time clock ran out, or it might seem? Neanderthal man was—and sad but true—cousins, aunts, and uncles having babies with each other. How long can that go on? As we will see, Charles Darwin was closer to answering this question than most of us ever want to be. His matrimony with his genetic cousin bears out the conflict with offspring conceived between relatives.

Science admits that they have found about three hundred un-fossilized remains around the world so I think it is fair to say that Neanderthal did in fact live in small groups. These groups left with dwindling genetic resources became extinct. Genetic diversity was just not available to them to continue as a species. Some claim that Neanderthals went extinct because their hips were not made for running, and they could not compete with the smaller weaker Homo sapiens that could run. Did our Neanderthal cousins have a genetic hip defect from long incidents of inbreeding? He mixed up his genes with relatives, which will lead to genetic malfunctions. Too bad they didn't have modern science to help them out. I think modern science still believes genetic diversity is good, right?

Let us look at an example of interbreeding with close relatives. It is interesting to note biblical law has certain moral and ethical rules to keep man from corrupting himself and his offspring. Our evolutionist friends see these laws as GOD's old book of fairy tales. Charles Darwin, the father of evolution, had a very interesting disagreement with the Bible, and it conflicted personally; he suffered the repercussions in his personal life.

Charles married his first cousin Emma Wedgwood. They had ten children. Wow, sounds like no harm, no foul, but closer investigation reveals that three of these children died before adolescence.

Annie Darwin died at the age of ten from scarlet fever; her sister Mary died just twenty-three days after being born. Brother Charles Warning Darwin died from scarlet fever as a toddler. The remaining seven children survived to adulthood but suffered many childhood illnesses. Six of the seven were married for many years, but only four of the seven Darwin kids produced children.

The other three of Charles children were apparently sterile, producing no children at all. This was compounded by the fact on the Wedgwood side of the family. Apparently, there were several marriages to cousins. A genetic union between relatives leads to a damaged immune system and a potential early death due to disease and, of course, causes sterility. This is a scientific fact not speculation; interbreeding leads to a genetic bottle neck.

Charles Darwin apparently studied the effect of interbreeding on plants and even tried to get an interbreeding question asked in the English census, but his efforts failed. He was aware of the problem in his own gene pool. Did this cause him to hate the GOD that expressly forbade his union with his cousin? I am not picking on Charles. He just represents an interesting question, is sex okay between close relatives? Rather, he came to the conclusion if it was wrong or not, we may never know. But given the consequences of his children's plight, it is well documented.

After all, the glaring fact is at some point in his life, he must have thought it perfectly fine. Having ten children bears this out. I am sure Charles knew of his predicament. Mr. Darwin must have heard of this concept; it was during the Victorian era, and religion was very popular. Could this union with his first cousin possibly be bad and have a detrimental effect to his offspring?

As Charles traveled, he studied plants and animals to understand how they reacted to their environment, and he may have thought of his situation as perfectly okay. He may have for a time thought he might be better off by producing children so close to the family tree. But in eighteenth century Europe, the atheist point of view was definitely in the minority. Is it possible Mr. Darwin suffered some chastisement or public ridicule? We may never know. But as I pointed out, his situation is clearly understood, and the union between cousins did happen. The consequence of the union between cousins is clearly demonstrated.

Annie Darwin was Born on March 2, 1841, and died at the age of ten (she may have had tuberculosis); she passed on April 23, 1851. It was the prolonged death of Annie that radically altered Darwin's belief in Christianity. Mary Eleanor Darwin, born on September 23, 1842, but died a few weeks later. Darwin's last child to die was Charles Waring Darwin, born on December 6, 1856, but died on June 28, 1858.

It may be pure conjecture, but it is safe to say Charles had seen the tragedy most of us never want to experience. These facts are important in discovering Mr. Darwin's mind-set. Nonetheless, it should be remembered; Darwin launched his new book while still suffering grief from the death of his son. By the time of the release of his most famous work, three of the ten Darwin children had already passed. Could it be that evolution was the hammer in which Charles struck at the GOD that created him?

In light of this deep and personnel tragic loss, *Origin of the Species* came out on November 24, 1859. It was an instant success, and it flew off the bookshelves. It became the first book in a new line of thought—"evolution." Is it possible Darwin thought his marriage to his cousin would work out fine? Perhaps Emma might have reassured Charles it was okay because after all, it had been practiced on her side of the family before.

Was there a science that could have prevented this terrible tragedy? As it turns out, yes, there was such a science. It was readily available to Charles and, in fact, other family members as well. The Holy Bible forbids such unions.

> None of you shall approach any one of his close relatives to uncover nakedness. I am the Lord. You shall not uncover the nakedness of your father, which is the nakedness of your mother; she is your mother, you shall not uncover her nakedness. You shall not uncover the nakedness of your father's wife; it is your father's nakedness.

> You shall not uncover the nakedness of your sister, your father's daughter or your mother's daughter, whether brought up in the family or in another home. You shall not uncover the nakedness of your son's daughter or of your daughter's daughter, for their nakedness is your own nakedness. (Lev. 18:6–16)

Accounts of how Moses determined these laws are certainly unclear. If GOD told this to Moses or he figured it out by the scientific method, the advice is certainly sound and applicable to this very day. Remember this, the scientific method is supposition, observation, and predictions of outcomes. "What?" Was Moses a scientist or just some poor moron plagued by his own superstition? Three thousand years later and it still works, and evolution can't fix it, because it was never broken. Any law no matter how simplistic has only one criterion—that it must be the truth.

Sounds like good advice to me, and I think science will bear out this fact. Can we all agree on the truthfulness of this fact? If you procreate too close to home, you might have genetic defects like a damaged immune system, causing childhood sicknesses and in the case of the Darwin family, three tragic but predictable deaths and sterility. His faith in GOD now deeply conflicted; the tragedy was probably more than he could bear. If he renounced his faith in GOD, the record is certainly unclear. None of us can judge Darwin for that is not up to us, but he did outline a possible world where in now Darwin had a competing idea in direct opposition to the Bible.

If Darwin was angry at GOD or not isn't up for debate, it wouldn't matter if he was. Charles, after watching the tragic loss of his children, provided the book that attempted to replace GOD with a new religion. The new atheist drive was on. Atheists provide evolution as their belief that there is no GOD, but tragically, evolution is a myth compounded with little or no evidence. Evolution became the vehicle that chipped and pounded those Bible thumpers into submission. Exhibits, books, and soon museums were heavily involved and needed fresh material. This was during the days of the freak shows, and competition was fierce for new exhibits especially in the newly established museums. The evolution temples exist today in the museums our kids visit to learn Earth Science. Children's curiosity is compounded by their interest in dinosaurs and oh, by the way, look at the caveman over there!

Charles was understandably hurt and turned that hurt on his GOD. After all, had Charles read his Bible, he may have come to the conclusion that he was complicit in his own tragedy and grief.

It is also possible he may have thought GOD had singled him out for some kind of personal torment, but we will just never know. For now, let's leave Mr. Darwin to his new religion and look at the result of it.

Java man: Initially discovered by Dutchman Eugene Dubois in 1891; all that was found of this claimed originator of humans was a skullcap, three teeth, and a femur. The femur was found fifty feet away from the original skullcap a full year later. For almost thirty years, Dubois downplayed the Wadjak skulls (two undoubtedly human skulls found very close to his "missing link"). (Source: Hanegraaff, Hank. *The Face That Demonstrates the Farce of Evolution*. Nashville: Word Publishing, 1998).

Mr. Dubois played down the fact that two human skulls were found in the same strata although sixty-five miles away. This places Java man with modern humans. The femur was human, and the teeth were from an orangutan. Not much to go on, but you can still look up Java man on the web. Java man had only one apparently artifact in question—the skullcap, which Mr. Dubois contemporaries concluded that the skullcap was from an extinct giant gibbon.

Evolutionist won't let it go, and Mr. Java still plays the nightclubs in evolutionary farce. They refer to it as definitely human. Please, if Mr. Java dated your sister, I don't think you could count on nieces and nephews. It is pertinent to remember that species can reproduce only with a genetically comparable mate to produce a viable offspring. Is a chimp a human? No. Gorilla? No. Orangutan? No. In the end, Eugene Dubois only had one flaw—he was not a real scientist. When confronted with the facts Mr. Java was a giant extinct gibbon, Eugene finally relented. Fake? No, just wishful thinking but a farce nonetheless. Evolutionists base their facts on the size of the skull as the final word, but like the truth, it must make sense.

Evolutionists refuse to believe Mr. Java could be a giant gibbon. In 1996, two mummified gibbons were found in China. It was estimated if standing upright, they would be over seven feet tall. Large skull capacity, nine hundred cubic centimeters; that would explain perfectly the large skullcap. Oh lest, we forget who mummified those giant extinct gibbons, real honest to goodness *humans*. (Source: "7 Foot Tall Giant Gibbons?" http://frontiersofzoology.blogspot.com)

Here we go again, mix and match bones to make what you want—a femur here, a scapula there—and there you have it, a real honest to goodness Australopithecus. Posing as a thinking man, his intellect tells the evolutionist let's keep what we want and throw the rest out. Fossil remains are found sometimes miles away from each other, but the thinking goes maybe a mudslide moved the bones and certainly, something must have moved in four million years. But this is a simple fix to a complex problem, and fossil finding sometimes are taken from a pretty large box. Cases of mistaken identity are commonplace. The real truth is, if you find fifteen fossils, are they from the same creature or fifteen different creatures? The finding of an adolescent body and the skullcap from an adult would produce a creature with what would appear to be a larger skull and oh yes old uncle Australopithecus. What Mr. Dubois found was really just one fossil a skullcap but from what?

"Piltdown Man," Charles Dawson was a believer in the new science, and apparently, a superior amateur archaeologist; he lived in the south of England near Sussex. Charles Dawson apparently found a skull in the Pleistocene gravel beds near Piltdown village in Sussex, England. Dawson teamed up with Arthur Smith Woodward, who was the curator of geology at the Natural History Museum.

Astonishingly, it was discovered that the fossils were five hundred thousand years old. This was determined by the expert Arthur Woodward and represented a long extinct human they dubbed Piltdown Man.

The most important part of the find included a partial skull and complete jawbone. Piltdown man made his debut in 1912 at the Geological Society. The reconstructed skull and jawbone were accepted as the most important find to date, and the evolutionary science was off and running.

For the next forty years, Piltdown man was studied and on display as a glaring testament to the truthfulness of the new science. As the evolution/religion dictates, the family albums and artwork appeared, and the world was amazed with the new find. Piltdown appeared in journals everywhere for years. Soon, the enthusiastic evolutionist found many new converts in light of virtually no scientific evidence for no other fossil remains were ever found. Here, we start with the idea Piltdown man or at least most of him must have washed away.

In 1949, a new method was used to determine the age of the most important find in evolutionary history. It was discovered that the date of Piltdown man's demise was only fifty thousand years ago.

Further investigation revealed the finding of the Piltdown man was an elaborate fake. The skull was of a modern man, and the jawbone belonged to what was most likely an orangutan with the teeth filed down to look human.

A total forgery, teeth filed to look human? Apparently, the fraud was complete right down to the stain on the bones to make them look like the color of the pit in which they were supposedly found. It will never be known if Arthur Smith Woodward was complacent in the fraud, but the evolutionist Charles Dawson definitely was. It was his discovery that led the way with fraud, deceit, and outright lies.

His invention was named after him *Eoanthropus dawsoni*. Of particular interest, that canine teeth that were missing from the fossil, they were later discovered in the same pit. Not only was it a hoax, it was a well-thought-out elaborate hoax, full of drama and intrigue. Dawson was quite busy and discovered several new fossil species *Salaginella dawsoni, Iguanodon dawsoni*, and *Plagiaulax dawsoni*. They were presented to Arthur Woodward and accepted as genuine. All considered fakes today. Whether Woodward knew it or not, he was an important part of the plot and gave the forgeries validation. Dawson was an artistic forger, an apparently duped not only Woodward but also the experts of the day.

In the end, Dawson fooled the so-called experts for over fifty-eight years. Piltdown man went extinct from the evolutionarily playbook in 1953, and his other three discoveries were determined to be manufactured fakes in the 1960s. It is ironic that in the end, Mr. Dawson died before being discovered. His reason for the fraud, it seems he wanted the title Sir Dawson, a knighthood, so he could rub elbows with the intellectuals of the day. His knighthood never happened, and in the end, Mr. Dawson received a title of sorts; if you google his name, *hoax* appears either after his name or near the Piltdown man his most elaborate fraud.

It should never be forgotten that Piltdown man was the centerpiece of evolutionary thought theory and practice for over forty years. It is safe to say that this being the case, evolution has a foundation of fraud from the very beginning. Evolutionists really don't like the Piltdown man exposé because it points to the basic concept that evolution has its roots placed firmly in fraud deception and outright lies.

"Nebraska Man" was discovered in 1922 by Harold Cook in the Pliocene deposits of Nebraska. A tremendous amount of literature was built around this supposed missing link, which allegedly lived one million years ago. The evidence for Nebraska Man was used by evolutionists in the famous Scopes (monkey) evolution trial in Dayton, Tennessee, in 1925. William Jennings Bryan was confronted with a battery of "great scientific experts" who stunned him with the "facts" of Nebraska Man. Mr. Bryan had no retort except to say that he thought the evidence was too scanty and to plead for more time. Naturally, the "experts" scoffed and made a mockery of him. After all, who was he to question the world's greatest scientific authorities? But what exactly was the scientific proof for Nebraska Man? The answer is a *tooth*. That's right; they found one tooth! The top scientists of the world examined this tooth and appraised it as proof positive of a prehistoric race in America. What a classic case of excessive imagination! Years after the Scopes trial, the entire skeleton of the animal from which the initial tooth came was found. As it turns out, the tooth upon which Nebraska Man was constructed belonged to an extinct species of pig. The entire pig found years later. The "authorities," who ridiculed Mr. Bryan for his supposed ignorance, created an entire race of humanity out of the tooth of a pig! What an embarrassment to the scientific community and a noteworthy commentary on evolutionary human nature. Needless to say, little publicity was given to the discovered error. Surely, there is a lesson here for us concerning the reliability of so-called "expert testimony," which is so often used to manipulate and intimidate the layman. A similar discovery, which was also based upon a tooth, was the Southwest Colorado Man. It is now known that this particular tooth actually belonged to a horse! How resourceful and imaginative scientific "experts" can be at times. Give them a tooth, not necessarily human, and they can create an entire race of prehistoric humanity. (Scott M. Huse, *The Collapse of Evolution*, pp. 97–98)

I could not say it any better than Mr. Huse so I didn't even try. I would like to point out the particular vindictiveness of the atheist/evolutionist the witness in the Scopes Monkey Trial. Williams Jennings Bryant was a giant in his day and even ran for the presidency of the United States three times. He was a congressman twice and United States Secretary of State under Woodrow Wilson. Bryant was treated like an imbecile by the so-called experts who had a reason for such an attack. Mr. Bryant was an expert on the Bible, a devout Presbyterian and an advocate against Darwinism based on his religious beliefs and humanitarian grounds. It was later discovered that the evolutionary experts of the day created an entire race of proto-humans from the tooth of an extinct pig!

Let's get back to our Neanderthal friends; they were able to overcome the hip defect because they were forest ambush hunters. They did not need to run, just ambush a deer running through the trees. Many scientists agree that Neanderthal DNA still exist in the chromosomes of modern-day Europeans and Asians alike. This agreement leads one to believe that Neanderthal may have procreated with Cro-Magnon Man (virtually us), and some of his DNA still survives today.

This hypothesis is hampered by the fact that a Cro-Magnon/Neanderthal procreation event could only go one way. Neanderthal man and Cro-Magnon female would produce a viable offspring but only if the child were a male. Females would be sterile and most probably end up in a still birth or a more likely an aborted fetus. Not good for the hybrid as his genetic makeup would soon be washed out by the Cro-Magnon gene pool. Female Neanderthal and male Cro-Magnon would most certainly end up as a sterile female, and if she could procreate, it would most likely end up not being able to procreate itself or it would die in adolescence.

There are those who hold on to the hope that Neanderthal had forty-eight chromosomes and we Homo sapiens have forty-six, is a procreation event possible? There are results found in the equine world, a horse and a donkey will produce a mule, and he will be sterile. Conjecture over this matter can be subjective as while it is a rule, there have been recorded sixty-one viable offspring in such unions. When compared to the three hundred Neanderthal skeletons found, we are on pretty thin ice to think this happened in any large numbers. Further investigation reveals that some scientists would like Neanderthal to have forty-eight chromosomes because chimps, gorillas, and orangutans do.

We have come to the crux of the matter, the magic number forty-eight; is this what ties our existence through Neanderthal to our closest living relative, the *chimp*? Not so fast. Apparently, in genetics, you can't go back. Genetic differences made the union of chimps with Neanderthals impossible. This is because while the numbers of the genes might possibly be the same, the makeup is so different that any offspring simply is impossible

Well, the fact is, we have been promised the missing link. Where is it? Neanderthal, yes, "that must be it." The problem is, the number and structure of Neanderthal DNA points to, in their view, forty-six because a two-chromosome chasm is a pretty far bridge to cross. Neanderthal was a cousin with a distant common ancestor to us. My question is forty-eight or forty-six, but common sense points to forty-six. A child with Down syndrome has forty-seven chromosomes, but they are still human—just a human with Down syndrome. The addition or deletion of a chromosome is no easy mean feat and has a host of problems that are too long to go over here, for examples of creatures changing the numbers in their genetic strands do not exist except in the rarest of cases.

Can we agree that there may be a possibility that forty-seven chromosomes produce an offspring with Down syndrome and a human with forty-eight chromosomes would produce a muscle-bound man from the waist up with the legs of a virtual cripple from the waist down? Science isn't even close to entertaining this possibility because they are too busy trying to find that elusive missing link. At the time of this writing, they are still looking but sadly no cigar. They have been looking and to date, the record doesn't look too good. They have been looking for 156 years now, and it appears they are no closer than when they started.

Can science tell us if what they are studying is a protohuman, a human, or a human with a genetic defect attained through inbreeding? Not an easy question to answer, is it? Neanderthal at best has proven no help in identifying or pointing to our genetic past. Could it be because Neanderthal was us or at the least genetically compatible?

The Max Plank Institute is mapping the genome of the Neanderthal, and most scientists virtually agree that they may have bred themselves into nonexistence. Was Neanderthal a virtual genetic bottle neck that led to their extinction? I don't think the Max Plank

Institute will be able to answer that question any time soon, because they are hung up on proving Homo sapiens is related to the chimp. Once you understand the subject more clearly, it is easily realized that jumping over this hurdle is virtually impossible, even for the Max Plank Institute.

If they have mapped the Neanderthal genome, then the 46–48 question should be easily answered. But for now, we can accept the Max Plank confession for genetic cousins. Is this the easy way of conceding the answer forty-six chromosomes for our genetic cousins? If it were forty-eight chromosomes, Max would be yelling from the rooftops.

They need to answer the question, can interbreeding through a millennium cause genetic deformations? The Bible warns against it. Just imagine trying to figure that one out. My guess is, it would be easier to prove, although it would be a loose conclusion to say Neanderthal is our distant cousin. Some geneticist think they are still with us today, and Europeans carry the Neanderthal genes with them to this day. Extinct? I wouldn't think so.

When one contemplates the reality of where did the Neanderthal come from, it is relatively easy to conclude that someone in the next county over was trying to duplicate GOD's miraculous feat by creating a creature to compete and, in the end, eradicate us humans. The argument between GOD and Satan we may not know or be able to understand, but it is clear that the approach to the construction of us humans and Neanderthal were very different.

Man was refined he loved; he felt passion and compassion, understood guilt, and he could think. Man's thinking was not just in the now but in the future also. In every sense of the word, us and with the hope in the divinity of GOD, man would find the perfection only GOD can provide for us. We like the GOD that created us have a soul.

Neanderthal was the perfect opposite and diabolically opposed to man in every way. He was not created to compete with us, or was he created to help and protect us. Neanderthal was created to destroy us any way he could by violence if need be or through procreation with our human women.

As every story of extinction has a moral to the story, alas so does the interaction between humans and Neanderthal. So here it is, Neanderthal was a mockery of GOD's greatest creation, and it was not man but woman who saved the genetic legacy of mankind. Women now GOD made her genetically perfect for the body of a human female, could produce countless generations of creatures from her genetic bloodline. She even had the ability to produce a human hybrid suitably able to establish and corrupt the bloodlines of man.

Neanderthal was created for only one vile reason—to destroy man. Should he (Satan) succeed, would he win his argument that man is really only after all just a fancy monkey? Satan has already lost, for he could not create a creature that both defied GOD's laws and tried to destroy his creation without a fatal flaw. While Neanderthal was created to destroy us, he was not created to last for millennia, for if he was, his female counterpart was seriously flawed even more than him.

It isn't conjecture or a wild guess to state without hesitation that female Neanderthal went extinct before the males did. There is no surviving genetic mitochondrial DNA from any female Neanderthal found in today's humans. Sadly, for Satan, his experiment was to prove GOD wrong, and his attempt to duplicate GOD's creation seriously flawed as Satan is flawed.

In essence, Satan hated us so much his own invention came with an expiration date, and it appears it was unknown to Satan. Satan's invention was on a one-way mission to destroy GOD's creation, man. How evil is evil; perhaps Satan's creation caused even fear in the entity responsible for its creation—Satan himself.

Imagine a great laboratory where test tubes filled with magic fluids made both creatures. Now imagine the truth GOD's finest creation woman defiled by Satan and his minions to destroy all of humankind. When you chase the lie out of your soul, the truth enters in. So we reach the truth, and it is this refusal to rejoice in the truth that can make us all a slave to the lie.

Contrary to the writing of this book, science has given away the information by not publishing the most important facts. Neanderthal is not extinct; he lives in the bodies of his genetic children to this day. Neanderthal did what humans do and in fact, all species do; he survived through procreation. The bottom line is, while evolution is treated as a science, it really is not. While it uses bits and pieces of the scientific method in collecting information, evolution is not observable or testable. It remains a 156-year-old bag of atheist wishful thinking and hype.

Despite what one might think, the weak and elusive facts are that evolution has had very rocky beginnings. As we will soon see, every discovery found either in a remote location in some far-flung jungle or as in the case of Mr. Dawson in his own backyard, the reality is, fraud is the hallmark of evolution's jagged and rusty beginnings.

Chapter 2

○

Archaeological Forgeries?

If there is fossil evidence to support the evolutionist theory, it is often constructed to proliferate the misguided conclusion that we are descendants from our ancestors—the chimps or the ape. With that fantasy and the help of artist rendering in their hands, evolutionist produce brutish creations that resemble half-ape, half-man creatures. The simple truth is, these drawings are simply just a fantasy of the evolutionist's imagination. If as the evolutionist contend Neanderthal went extinct forty thousand years ago, how could anyone know what they looked like?

From a single bone a family album appears, with the family enjoying a meal or running from the local saber-tooth tiger; you know, trying to avoid the problem with being on the menu. They produce what they would like you to believe, what it was like to be alive a million years ago. After all, seeing is believing, isn't it? Oh yeah, all of this from just one bone.

Evolutionists often produce plenty of art to get you to believe. This is taught in the classrooms, and it is a popular subject with kids who are also fascinated with dinosaurs and the cavemen. The indoctrination begins at an early age to give the kiddies a chance to see what life was really like for the 2 percent a million years ago. But it is either the truth or it isn't. It still remains just a theory and other than fertilizing the minds of children, it is still really just fertilizer.

Children become disillusioned when they find that dinosaurs and cavemen never existed during the same time period, thoughts of the Flintstones riding brontosaurus disappears from their little minds. Young impressionable minds get used to the concept and if we can throw a little atheist/agnostic disbelief in there, what's the harm? It is taught in schools and the inevitable outcome is, it is a reason to doubt not just GOD, but his most elaborate creation, man. It isn't easy to conceptualize history and understand extinction events, but evolutionists draw a fine line between causes for these extinction events as we will see.

Archaeologists—run mostly by real scientists—can produce dinosaur eggs, or a complete skeletal fossil of a dinosaur no bigger than a chicken. But the rarest creature of all is a complete fossilized primordial man. What are we saying here exactly? That an egg or a small dinosaur that died sixty million years ago is found and on display at the local museum. While complete skeletal fossils of protohumans are just so rare complete skeletal remains just don't exist. After 156 years, they haven't discovered the complete skeletal remains of just one. Remember this, some finds are as scanty as a single tooth and have been used to propagate the implausible, improbable, and inconclusive concept of evolution.

When it comes to our cave brothers who died half a million years ago, fossils are extremely rare, and the feet are seldom present. If the feet are present, they are always a problem; if evolution was real, then the transition of the big toe would be clearly demonstrated. If it were a protohuman, then the foot and position of the big toe could date the correct age these protohumans lived in. All of this depends on the position of the big toe on the chimp's foot/hand thingy. Humans have hands and feet; the great apes have hands and hands. This is a bridge too far and not easily explained by even the experts.

Evolutionists haven't even produced a protohuman with so much as a bunion to explain the human foot anomaly, just too rare, I guess. They do mix and match placing the big toe to make it look like it is trying to turn into a human foot, but the reality of this cannot hide the fact that human feet are completely unique. The truth is that while fossilized human feet are found, they are always found on human remains. Assertions that it just happened over time leave little or no evidence of such an event now or ever.

The modality of the human foot is fascinating at least and a miracle at best. The human foot requires a large heel bone to support the entire weight of the human body. In addition to that, it must walk; something gorillas, chimps, and orangutans cannot do efficiently, so they don't walk at least not under normal circumstances. Their efficiency is hampered because their heel bones are too small, their feet are too small, and their hips are too small. The great apes do not use walking as their usual mode of transportation because it is just so inefficient for them. The great ape's foot has no arch or a big toe to cushion the impact of his body weight.

But if you give them (evolutionist) enough bones, they can come up with anything. Remember, hominid fossils are always found with human fossils. If you gave them enough bones, they could come up with a chimp's foot in a set of Nike basketball shoes. Problem here is, they are just too rare. The magic of the human foot is incredible to comprehend. The heel hits the ground, the outer pad of the foot comes in contact with the ground, traverses forward, and the entire weight of the body shifts to the big toe. This bipedal motion propels us forward again and again. Look at the ballerina who can walk on the tip of her big toes alone. The great apes better not try that at home. To our atheist friends, Australopithecus couldn't do it either; he had no butt to hold up his lower spine and absorb the impact of walking, for after all, a chimp is just a chimp.

Chimps and gorillas have a big toe that extends from the arch of what would be a human foot. Evolutionists claim that the bones of the foot are too small and decay through time very quickly. Really, an egg can survive sixty million years, but a foot can't survive half a million years. "Yea, sure." The identification is difficult at best when major identifying parts are missing and surely to the logical mind inconclusive.

Lucy is a great example. The skeleton found in 1974 was almost 40 percent complete, and her feet were zero percent complete, not one toe. Evolutionists will always look at the head for identification, even the smallest bit or a piece of a skull, and artists are working on the new caveman family album. The problem here is, almost all creatures have a skull, and fossilized remains give little clues as to where or what they came from.

Baboon, pigs, and donkeys have all been mistaken for our primal relatives. The truth is, if you found a protohuman who could hang from his feet from a tree, then it wouldn't be a human. "Would it?" The simple truth is, humans (Homo sapiens) have two thumbs and two big toes. Apes and chimps have four thumbs, two on the hands and two on the feet. Pretty severe adaptions to be accomplished for even for half a million years of evolution. Actually, the foot of a chimp looks more like a hand than it looks like a human foot.

If there aren't any such fossils, then let's just manufacture the fossils. Oh, but that pesky foot, common sense tells us that if we evolved through millennia, then the big toe would make a gradual transition from the middle arch of the foot to the front and slowly produce the modern human foot. Hanging by your feet from trees, it appears, is less difficult than finding one transitional bipedal walking protohuman foot. So any evolutionary discovery that has been fossilized is your great-great-aunt Ethyl or Uncle Bert. This assumption is absurd, and the resemblance of Australopithecus to the modern chimps is a much closer match to both of these creatures than modern humans to either species.

We could theorize that through mutation, it happened rather quickly. There is just one problem with that theory, folks. What structures were manipulated in the gene pool to go from a swinging hand into a walking foot? The chances of any creature receiving the same genetic mutation at the same time and finding a genetically suited companion are in the billions. But what about all that artwork? Even body mechanics are an insurmountable task to overcome, for no other creature in nature now or ever has changed its method of body transportation. Why would they?

Evolutionists, meet the mathematicians. Simple numbers should indicate the plausibility of compatible genetic change, but the odds of such an event are none. Evolutionary thought cannot comprehend the chances of genetic change over the millions of years they say it happened. They still insist it happened, but where is the proof? According to the theory, slow kinds of evolutionary change take millions of years to take place, but we humans and chimps stand alone in the evolutionary ladder to change body mechanics.

The human foot is an absolute miracle. Without it, we couldn't walk upright, at least not for very long. If you have ever seen a chimp walk on two legs, it looks painful. According to the body structure of the chimp, bipedal locomotion is not possible, and the conflict is apparent. How could it not hurt? Imagine the entire weight of a full-grown man on the flat feet of a ten-year-old boy; the lower leg muscles holding the entire body up at the lower spine. The strain compresses the vertebrae trying to hold the upper torso and no butt to help take the shock. In a simple word, impossible at best and an unlikely random act of genetic restructuring at the worst.

It is rather easy to see that a walking chimp, gorilla, or orang-utan looks very much like a cripple trying to accomplish a task that its body was never made to accommodate. They don't do it. As a matter of fact, they only do it as a matter of necessity and only when walking on two legs is the only option for them. They are literally performing what for them is an elaborate balancing act. If you ever worked in a zoo and taught chimps to do that, you should be arrested for cruelty to animals.

The evolutionist believes they did it for a million years so they could invent a god. Now, who is the imbecile? The transition from the quadrupedal gorilla to bipedal man must have been miraculous. Whatever it was that caused them to walk upright, who knows. The reasonable question would be, why would an animal change its loco-motion in the first place? The real answer is, they didn't.

Successful species change out of necessity according to the the-ory, and the evolutionist forget that Darwin taught natural selection also. What drove Australopithecus to walk? This is a reasonable ques-tion, but this question is never really answered. While walking in a bipedal manner has its advantages, imagine humans walking on all fours. This locomotion doesn't work for humans because our body structure will fight this impulse because it doesn't work for us.

Natural selection is probably the only redeemable part of Darwinism; nature will not choose to change a successful species, why would it? If this is true, why would successful apes, chimps, or orangutans choose to change their genetic structure? There are three great apes (chimpanzee, gorillas, and orangutans), five species of baboons (lesser apes), twelve species of gibbons, 120 species of monkeys, and only one species of man. On the overall scale from one to ten, I would say our primate friends are doing okay despite having no help from us humans.

Archaeological digs are littered with the bones of everything, including your true genetic ancestors, "man." Mix and match looks good on the news, but a human foot on a tree swinging chimp is laughable. If you throw in the skullcap of a giant baboon, hello, now you got something. The bits and pieces thrown together equate to wearing a clown, cop, and fireman costume to a Halloween party. You won't win any prizes because clown, cop, and fireman don't really exist and neither does Java man, Peking man, or Nebraska man. What do exist are Java baboon, Peking chimp, and Nebraska pig, and that is the truth for nothing else makes any sense.

The evolutionist would have you believe that all those feet changed over millennia very slowly; something they can't prove. But the reality points to overnight as the fossil record yields few fossils to make their point of slow transitional evolutionary change. If it is to be believed at all, it should be expected that this anomaly must be explained for evidence to prove it happened doesn't exist. This would explain a lot but isn't in the evolution playbook because it just isn't there. If, as the evolutionist claims, that "man created GOD," then is it fair to say "evolutionist created evolution?" It is an elaborate constantly changing story full of holes that need to be patched up on occasion, but if you were wrong yesterday, what makes them right today?

Since evolutionists present much of their finds so clearly a child could see it. "Look at all the artwork!" We should remind them we are not children and are suspect of hoaxer's comic book heroes and, yes, artist concepts of their own imagination. We are in fact tired of the charlatans and deceivers who have invented a science that attempts to—through smoke and mirrors—explain the nonexistence of the GOD we believe in.

To the 73 percent of real scientists, do you want science to couple with fantasy, the voodoo plaguing the truth of your profession? This is not unlike the drunk guy with the lampshade on his head at a party. It's funny but only because it's embarrassing for everyone except the guy wearing the lampshade, he should be embarrassed but isn't. But with the lampshade firmly in place, it is difficult to see where they are going, and it appears they don't know themselves. The problem with embarrassment is, it turns to humiliation after a while. Is over 156 years long enough with a lampshade on their head to where it's getting humiliating yet?

In fact, they base their conclusions on fantasy, and often as in the case of Nebraska man, a single tooth from an extinct pig. All new scientific evolutionary discoveries are either a fraud or a case of mistaken identity. Early discoveries of extinct hominids are fabrications of bits and pieces of bone, incomplete skullcaps, and fantasy. The story goes from what if, to imagine that, to look at this. Childish!

Let's not forget those artist drawings that made a man from a single pig's tooth. This is astonishingly more miraculous than anything in the Bible by far. When it was discovered that it was a hoax, Nevada man drawings disappeared. Really very sad, but the evolutionists made them reappear for the next find to redeem their new science.

This fabrication alone is laughable, and the history of evolution is full of charlatans and hoaxers. Most of the names they give their imaginary friends are still found today. One good thing about evolutionists is, they recycle the names even when they are proven a fraud. This is obviously out of respect for those who duped us with their fantasy for generations before. They even rename their imaginary friends, and without apology for their last hoax, they promise, "This time, we got it right!" Because we have examined the last hoax, and now it is new and improved.

"Those extinct hominids" if you give them a Greek sounding name, and the harder it is to say, the more convincing it will be. To this day, evolutionary/science was and still relies on ignorance, deception, and fantasy. The only thing that has changed are the names. Sometimes, they are much more colorful these days, obviously making their fantastic claims just that more convincing. Let us stick to the facts and see where we end up.

> Gorillas have larger muscles in their arms than in their legs (the opposite is true for humans). This is primarily due to the fact that they use their increased arm strength for bending and gathering foliage and for defense. Although capable of walking upright on two feet, they most often walk as a quadruped (on four limbs). (Source: seaworld.com, see gorilla physical characteristics)

Wow (the opposite is true for humans), these mechanics are not like a deer, cheetah, or even cow. The gorilla leaps, lands on his knuckles, and swings his lower body forward. Not a very human thing to do, but it works for gorillas. People move by swinging their arms forward, propelling the two legs forward one at a time over a perfectly adapted spine and pelvis and move wherever they want. "Go team, go."

If you ever need to outrun an ape, you are in trouble. He will get you in short distances. So the genetic need for speed clearly makes no sense. The assertion being that adaptations are improvements, but losing strength and speed clearly demonstrate it wasn't very prudent for our ape friends to give up two vitally important and life-prolonging physical traits. Over the long haul, humans will be miles away if we get a head start. Should a gorilla catch you, those arms will pull you apart like a salad chef pulling apart a head of lettuce. What in the genetic instructions would give up strength for weakness in a world where strength was a perquisite for survival? The answer is obvious—it didn't happen. Evolutionary assertions that it did are, on the whole of it, ridiculous at the least and pure fantasy at best.

Last time I did the leg press, I could press 720 pounds. Don't try that at home with your arms. I am not exceptionally strong, just exceptionally human. The mechanics between humans and chimps are astoundingly different, and the complexities to join the two together are enormous. Why would any species give up an adaptation that makes you a veritable dissecting machine? Even the lion would be discouraged once his tail was pulled off or his skull crushed. But being slow made real humans, as it would appear easy prey for most predators, and so why are we still here?

The evolutionist wants you to believe we gave it up for much better things. "Like what, pizza?" Most weightlifters would never give up an adaption like that. But apparently, the weightlifter ancestors did? Ha! It appears that between the two, we are the most efficient at moving in bipedal fashion, and you might question why? In genetics, "you know real science," it appears that while humans have their strongest limbs in the legs, apes have the strongest limbs in their arms. "What?"

Evolutionist really! Genetics reversed course one day, and bodily mechanics changed overnight? All this coupled with a timeline of plus or minus three million years. Arms and legs reversed course from our closest living relatives, darn! Where are the fossils that show that incredibly slow transition? For a species to be successful, they must be able to proliferate in large numbers. Remember the three-thousand-year-old Leviticus rule? "Yea, I knew you would." No hanky-panky with kin. If you don't follow this rule, your kind will go extinct pronto. Out of all creatures, the most likely to change would be a creature known to live in large groups, not the small social groups of incestuous primates.

Out of the ten Darwin children, only four procreated. That won't get your species very far, or for very long. If you do that too many times, you will find the drooling, sterile, creation you are looking for complete with skeletal deformities. Where is the proof that this special transitional protohuman changed? They were so successful; in fact, as a genetic species, their line ended and they turned into us humans. With the facts clearly defined, where is the fossil proof? Oh, I know they are so hard to find. But on your digs, you shovel human bones out of the way so you can worship an extinct gibbon or an inbred chimp with a skull deformity. Remember, this deformity between biological relatives many times lead to skull deformation, just look at the pharaohs, need I say anything else? It is a fact that we know for sure the royal house of the pharaohs was an incest pool of who knows who in which fathers, sisters, mothers, and sons producing offspring with considerable deformation issues.

I mean, you could search the four corners of the earth. Sorry, you know what I mean—mix and match bones until you created such a creature. This is exactly what happens as we will see. But bones from Asia might need to be mixed with bones from Africa to furnish that hoax. Evolutionist would never do a thing like that ever! But I bet it sure is tempting—so tempting fossils are reconstructed from other finds elsewhere and assumed to be correct even from two different individuals from separate geographical parts of the world.

In incidents where two different animals from different areas of the world are used to explain the species' relevance, it does prove a link between two different animals and does little to explain any connection to man whatsoever. The real reason has no casual or causal answers to even the simplest questions of evolution and cannot be easily answered. What are the advantages of a walking chimp? The answer is simple and straight forward. Absolutely none. If it doesn't make any sense, then why should we consider it as truth!

If given enough puzzle pieces, the evolutionist could come up with a painting of the Mona Lisa complete with Leonardo's signature. The archaeological record supports the Bible, not evolution. Be fruitful and multiply and with seven billion people on the globe, we have done just that. So exactly why are protohuman fossils so darn hard to find? You may ask. Well, as it turns out, it is because common sense tells us chimps, gorillas, and orangutans' fossils are also just so hard to find. If genetic change were to occur, it would favor large numbers of creatures constantly breeding, competing for survival and adapting. But evolutionists have chosen a creature that lives in small groups, simply because they have arms and legs. This theory has chosen a creature small in numbers with no reason to change body structure body mechanics or even most importantly mental capacity.

The next time you are in a museum, ask to see the fossils of a chimp, gorilla, or an orangutan. Unfortunately, they will point to the protohuman exhibit. Yes, it's that stupid to them all primates are our ancestors. This is because all of those fossils are so rare they are all being used to try and convince us we are related to the great apes. While these creatures exist, it is embarrassing to make note of the fact that the hoax of evolution cannot explain why one out of the four species would decide to change and rather drastically its entire body structure. There is, however, a rather simple explanation to this also, because it simply didn't happen.

Evolutionary theory has a mathematic component not easily answered. As you would think, if genetic structures were manipulated, it would be much easier to accomplish any genetic manipulation if the numbers of creatures manipulated were greater in number. This explains why it did not happen because gorillas, chimps, and orangutans live in small groups and also die in small groups and like Australopithecus, they are difficult to find. Australopithecus is a common ancestor to the chimp and bears no physical relevance to modern man in the past or in the present.

Evolution is just a fanciful handful of conjecture speculation and old fossilized bones of mostly chimps and gorillas with the occasional horse pig or baboon thrown in for good measure. Every speculation into the origins of man other than GOD is met with conflicts in the theory of evolution itself. Do you really believe drastic and I mean drastic changes in body development happened over millions of years in small groups of ten to twenty individuals? Let us ask a simple question, did chimps look like mice five million years ago? My bet is the chimp looked like a chimp always, and his ancestor was Australopithecus, not related at all to humans.

This line of thinking is impossible, improbable, and in a word, purely a deluded fantasy. It is not GOD's plan that you should be deceived but believe in the truth. GOD has given man the intellect to triumph over all the ridiculous hype and even more act on those things you know to be just and true. To worship chimp fossils is a folly no one should endure if you have a good mind and question the science for it makes no sense.

If you came from the chimp, you are really just an animal and what rights does an animal have? Therefore, some would have you believe you are just an animal, but if a GOD created you, then you can count on hope, love, and be a social creature with the belief for all mankind that through the power of our minds, we can thrive together. Intelligence is worthless if it isn't used intelligently. To the date of this writing, any war in the future would lead to the extinction of us all. What is the antidote to this dilemma? Stop killing!

The concept of GOD is a virtue, for it is a path to perfection and the truth, for as we would expect GOD to be perfect, the perfection of science is and always has been a quest for the truth. A raccoon will never be a human, but if evolution were the truth, the raccoon would have an advantage over the chimp for a completely honest reason—the raccoon has hands and feet, not hands and hands like the chimp.

Evolution does have a purpose though. It wastes precious time and only serves to worship our illusionary ancestors. Man or chimp, it doesn't matter really, because it serves the purpose for which it was intended. To worship anything but the GOD who created everything! You can worship a half-man, half-ape living in a dank cave a million years ago but fail to see it as the hoax it really is. It is not as you would expect telling little lies to get you to believe the big lie; evolution is telling the biggest lie in the history of mankind—to get you to believe the little ones also. After all, you are really just a fancy chimp not that uncommon and to some, apparently, easily manipulated.

If the evolutionary model proves anything, it proves man has inserted an evolutionary point of view that is plagued with the prenotion that protohumans existed; they just can't find any. The ones they do find are so incomplete that 40 percent is a miraculous find indeed. But would any human put his destiny or that of his children in the hands of a 40 percent bet? The evolutionary gamblers not only do it on a daily basis, but also gamble with the souls of your children, too.

Perhaps there is nothing to find, because they never existed. Like Mr. Charles Dawson, not to be mistaken for Charles Darwin, Dawson invented the first anthropoid ever found, the fossils turned out to be a fraud. If Mr. Dawson had taken the time to find a real job, like let's say a paleontologist, he might have found the skull of a chimp, and we would have figured out the evolutionary hoax decades ago. Oh, but no, Mr. Dawson founded the parameters for truly deceiving those people who would accept it as truth or labeling those stupid that would rightly disagree. Thanks for the fraud, Mr. Dawson, you set the framework for evolution—lies, deceit, and water-colored paintings.

As it turns out, Piltdown man was totally manufactured from two separate species. Piltdown had a human skull with the jawbone of an orangutan. Let's talk about blind faith, folks. The realization is this, they are blinded from both the truth and the facts. You might say, come on now; after all, it is a free country. Okay, I give in; they win. Let's let them just keep worshipping the scattered bones of an ancient animal. The rest of us can join the clown, cop, fireman's union, but the evolutionist must pay our initiation dues. Guess what, if you believe in evolution, you have deceived yourselves!

This is truly a shame, and evolution is just animal worship dressed up in fanciful window dressing, sad but true. Is evolution a science? Many people think that it is; some claim it is an earth science. This is because that is the entry point for its teaching in school. But let's have a closer look at what science really is. I would like to point to the fact that for evolution to be a science, we need to change all the other sciences to exclude one or more of the following:

- Observations: Describing or measuring what one observes.
- Hypothesis: A statement that can be tested so that inferences and conclusions can be explained.
- Fact: Based on repeated observations that can be confirmed.
- Theory: A general explanation into which facts and experimental conclusions can be incorporated, so as to allow for predictions to be made.
- Law: A functional generalization that has stood the test of time and can be relied on to make accurate predictions.

(Source http://www.creationstudies.org/Education/is_evolution_science.html)

Observations: Description of animal fossils resembling a chimp more than a human.
Hypothesis: The chimps turned into a human? They just did. I said so, and I am smarter than you.
Fact: I have seen several reconstructed chimp fossils, and I am sure they are human ancestors. I said so, and I am smarter than you.
Theory: There is no GOD, so we came from chimps. I said so, and I am smarter than you.
Law: There is no GOD, so we came from chimps. I said so, and I am smarter than you.

Now we see why evolution will never be a science or be a law because no matter how you look at it, there are no answers provided by the so-called experts except (I said so, and I am smarter than you). So we can clearly see that the theory of evolution revolves around two facts: (1) There is no GOD, and (2) we came from chimps because I said so, and I am smarter than you. For those of you who feels like you must be missing something, don't feel alone; the other 98 percent are missing it also. Let's be fair and explain what we do know.

Observations: Description of an animal fossil resembling a chimp must be a chimp ancestor.
Hypothesis: The chimps cannot be turned into a human. No evidence exists to support otherwise.
Fact: I have seen several reconstructed chimp fossils, and I am sure they are chimps.
Theory: There is a GOD. No other evidence exists to explain the human anomaly. Evolution is therefore a hoax.
Law: There is a GOD because he is smarter than us, and he put us here.

All evolutionists have the unshakeable belief that because there is no GOD, we man exists as a creature of evolution, constantly changing into the creature that we are today. Well, really now? Left only with fossilized bones that cannot be carbon dated and because rock yields no DNA. Any assertions of the evolutionary origins of man prove impossible to verify or confirm, and it is, has, and will always be a theory in the minds of the self-deluded and self-convinced. The end result is a belief rooted in fossilized unverifiable poppy cock. All examples of protohuman are, in fact, extinct chimps, gorillas, and baboons.

Just because you find the fossilized bones of an anthropoid doesn't mean he is related to you. Not any more than liking peanuts makes you friends with the elephants at the local zoo. That clown, cop, fireman costume won't get you anything better than last prize at a Halloween party. Sorry, kids. To the evolutionist, it doesn't really matter, because their logic is that because we all evolved from anthropoids; we are related to anthropoids through some form or fashion because there is no GOD.

But what is the real truth? You made it all up, I would say, if I wasn't interested in the truth. The real facts are the evolutionist isn't clever enough to make up this evolutionary fairy tale. It isn't new thinking, for it has been believed for melena by the pagan cults throughout history. The belief in evolution will eventually end up where it always ends up—babies die and murder runs rampant, for it cheapens life and gives us an excuse to be animals. Some of us would prefer to believe that what we fill our bodies with spiritually follows us into the next life, and if it is good, we are filled with good and if it is bad, then we are lost. But there is hope for even the lost, however groveling at the feet of an extinct chimp, isn't it, friends?

Children want to be like their parents. They look up to us and rely on us for everything and in that fact alone points to a GOD of perfection, hope, and eventually, the truth. GOD loves us and cares for us. What possesses him to love us is so simple; it passes under the noses of most intelligent people. For GOD blew the breath of life in Adam and when He looks at us, He sees himself in us. The dragon (Satan), on the other hand, sees a chimp a clever monkey to be manipulated and so just really another animal. Any speculation on where evolution comes from is easily realized when you find the truth. Satan says we are chimps, and evolutionists believe it. The sad and total truth is the dragon says it, and the evolutionist really can't prove it, for it is a lie they have swallowed hook, line, and sinker.

The father of lies has spoken it to the evolutionists so often they desperately seek to prove it. The fact remains Satan has given evolutionists the task of proving the improvable, and sadly, a cruel task driving them to madness. Devil worship and witchcraft are much easier to contend with for they rely on the biggest lie of all—the dragon can save you when the truth is, he can't even save himself for he is eternally lost.

When declaring certain improvable anomalies as fact because of one's own perceived intelligence, evolutionists should consider that there is another science that describes evolutionary practitioners' thought process.

> Obsessive-compulsive disorder (OCD) is characterized by repetitive, unwanted, intrusive thoughts (obsessions), and irrational, excessive urges to do certain actions (compulsions). Although people with OCD may know that their thoughts and behavior don't make sense, they are often unable to stop them.
> (Source: "Obsessive-Compulsive Disorder." NAMI: National Alliance on Mental Illness. https://www.nami.org/learn-more/mental-health-conditions/obsessive-compulsive-disorder)

But what is bad business for the evolutionist is, there are human fossils that are found with so-called protohuman humans. We know this because human fossils are thrown out of the collection all the time. Lucy is a prime example, but more on her later. The evolutionists date these fossils according to the belief that protohuman existed first, so without any verifiable dating method, they just assign erroneous dates, really a best guess. Science, who knew? But is it science? No! It is evolutionary theory, and evolutionary theory is basically this. I said so, and I am smarter than you because there is no GOD.

The evolutionist, in general, adds as fact the presumptive conclusion that because we are hominids, we come from chimps. The evolutionary dating of fossils is extremely presumptive. If anthropoid fossils are found in the same strata of earth with human fossils, the monkey fossils are automatically dated as older. Carbon dating is impossible because you can't carbon date a rock. The evolutionary theory is just as unverifiable as which came first, the chicken or the egg?

The answer is grander and more exhilarating than the evolutionist can imagine. GOD came first! The grand creator, GOD, not only made the chicken and the egg, but He also made them to procreate innumerable times and unchanged just as they are. If anyone is infuriated by my claim that religion is a science, then let's look at one of its laws. Don't produce children with relatives. It is a law because it is observable testable, and proven results can be achieved by watching the results of it, and the outcomes are definitely predictable. Evolution, on the other hand, can produce none of the results of a law attained over thousand years ago by a guy named Moses.

This is a fact provable and verifiable, just ask Mr. Darwin. You could argue against it as much as you want, but believe it or not, not only is incest avoidance a verifiable law, but it's also against the law. Evolution is a collection of fairy tales, old bones, and a heavy slathering of wishful thinking. It has been trying to be a science since the first fake discovery by Mr. Dubois and displayed as proof positive since 1891. Fake? Yes!

Recently, a politician ran for the presidency of the United States and to boost her polling numbers, made the assertion that anyone who would vote for her political rival would be counted in the deplorable column. This would have been a major error in thinking had it not been for the fact she made it worse by describing what she thought was deplorable was, and you guessed it, they were most Christian and Jewish values. We all know the outcome for the impossible happened, and she lost. She later used the excuse that she lost the election because white husbands told their white wives how to vote a sorry commentary for a woman who ran for the presidency on the power of women.

The point here is, evolutionist describes Christians and Jews alike as deplorable; most of these people you would not let use your restroom. But Christian and Jewish values would let them in to do their business, while evolutionary values would leave them to do their business outside! All this so they could commune with the nature of the unnatural world of a theory impossible to prove. It is not the lie of probably, but the probability of the lie that separates those of us who believe in the certainty of the soul, and a kind and loving GOD and those who worship cold dead things without any proof.

Chapter 3

○

Lucy

In the words of that famous Homo sapien Ricky Ricardo, "Lucy, I'm home." Then we have Lucy, Donald Johanson discovery (circa 1974); fascinating creature and 40 percent complete. Give or take, a vertebra or a human toe! The chance discovery by Johanson is explained in full detail.

Johanson recollects, "I happened to glance over my right shoulder...and there on the surface of the ground was a little bit of an elbow. I recognized it immediately as belonging to a human ancestor" (Source: ice.org. "Was Lucy an Ape-man?" by John D. Morris, PhD).

And there I was in a junk yard, and I could see a lug nut, and I knew instantly it was a blue green 1956 Chevy 283 ragtop with an automatic transmission. "Don't you know guys like that?" "I don't either, but it looks like they exist in evolutionary circles though." If that made you laugh, perhaps it is because you are not an evolutionist. If you are an evolutionist and laughed, perhaps you have finally noticed the lampshade on your head.

Lucy, it appears, is an Australopithecus; the head appeared to be that of a gorilla. And according to Dr. John D Morris and I quote:

> From the neck down, nearly every feature was
> likewise nonhuman. Australopithecus fossils,

including those which are thought to be much more recent and therefore should be more humanlike, have long, curved fingers and long, curved toes—well adapted to swinging from tree limb to tree limb.

The Creation Museum model of Lucy shows how the original Australopithecus afarensis fossils support the knuckle-walking habits of this extinct ape. Additional bones clearly associated with afarensis specimens support this ape's arboreal lifestyle by revealing features such as wrist bones that lock for knuckle-walking and shoulder blades oriented for swinging in the trees. Image: Answers in Genesis Creation Museum, Petersburg, Kentucky

(Source: https://answersingenesis.org/human-evolution/lucy/lucy-makeover-shouts-a-dangerously-deceptive-message-about-our-supposed-ancestors/)

Dr. Charles Oxnard completed the most sophisticated computer analysis of australopithecine fossils ever undertaken and concluded that the australopithecines have nothing to do with the ancestry of man whatsoever and are simply an extinct form of ape (Source: *Fossils, Teeth, and Sex: New Perspectives on Human Evolution.* University of Washington Press, 1987). Stern and Sussman write in the American Journal of Physical Anthropology (60:279–313).

"Look at the feet on that girl." Yes, conspicuously not there. "Monkey feet, monkey feet." Sorry, no feet, just one toe. The toe was apparently removed when it was discovered it was human. But that toe does appear in some reconstructed art, and it appears Lucy had human feet in the artwork not demonstrated by any evidence whatsoever. Any artistic rendering of a Lucy with human feet are a fraud simply because other specimens of a Lucy-type creature with human feet are nonexistent.

Apparently, because of past frauds, many anthropologists are given the opportunity to examine the new finds. They may give their blessing to the new find or discredit it. Due to their professionalism and frauds of the past, they do try and find dissimilarities because like the Scopes Monkey Trial and Piltdown man, no scientist wants to be labeled a rube even after they have passed on. So it would appear some people still have the courage to find the truth, even and especially real scientists.

Lucy, it seems, is very important because she is the most complete reconstruction in the fossil record. To date, some of the vertebrae have been removed and possibly the only toe bone found with the old girl. This was because it was from a human, and yes, it was fossilized. Fossilization takes millions of years, doesn't it? No. If the right conditions exist, it can happen in a matter of years. They have found fossilized work boots in old abandoned mines.

It is interesting to note Lucy's age was determined by radiocarbon dating from some ash found close to her fossilized remains. If you are impressed, you shouldn't be. Human fossils were also discovered close to Lucy's remains also. What would the ash from the same pit prove if found next to human fossils? "Nothing?" It is a fact even human bones were inadvertently placed with her fossilized record. Apparently, they really didn't want to know! While Lucy is determined to be extremely ancient, the human fossilized bones were not assigned any date simply because everyone knows Australopithecus came before chimps and people because you see, there is no GOD. Do you see the lie and how it works? If in the human fossils they found a piece of ash that proved the human remains were older than Lucy case closed! You see how it works; it is a wild guess based on the assumption that despite the absence of knowing the truth, it helps to bend the data to prove their point. The reality is this, it only serves to prove that the evolutionist bends data or makes it up completely and hides the rest! Author emphasis added...

The evolutionist could also cast doubt on the history of man from a biblical perspective if the two sets of human fossils were proven to be a million years old, for the Bible says otherwise. Their logic is twisted so much because they cannot tolerate not being in control of the narrative. If you don't smell a rat, then you don't understand; not only can there be no questioning about basic logic from evolutionists simply because there is no GOD!

> Since 1974, however, more bones have been recovered from other members of Lucy's species. Her toes have been shown to curve like tree-dwelling apes; her shoulders have been found to be nearly identical to living great apes; her wrists resemble those of other knuckle-walking ape species; and her hands—far from being like human hands—are similar to those of chimpanzees. In other words, she was an ape—a tree-climbing, knuckle-walking, amazingly designed ape. (Source: "Lucy: Did She Walk Like Us?" answersingenesis.org)

Any assertion that fossilization takes millennia is just ridiculous. Finding animal fossils and determining which is older, chimp fossils or human fossils, points to the fact that you just will never know. But there is a fifty-fifty chance if you pick one, you might be right. Evolution, who knew? Not much to go on for believing the lie requires you to give up your eternal existence on "I said so, and I am smarter than you." Remember, taking advice from people who claim to have no soul sounds like a story out of a witchcraft movie and so it really is.

What good old Don found was an Australopithecus, at least the body was, with the exception of a leg bone, which some surmise came from a four-year-old human girl and, yes, fossilized. The leg bone was the most convincing evidence for walking upright, but Donald found it three kilometers away and two hundred feet deeper than Lucy. It appears either the leg bone wasn't hers, or the old girl really got around even after she died. Imagine the work involved in finding a leg bone two hundred feet below the ground and for what—it only proved a human child lived the same time Lucy did. Where is your evolution now?

Without that leg bone, Lucy was just an old-fashioned girl with a propensity for swinging in the trees. Ah, but with that leg bone, she was a star. She was a pi up girl for *National Geographic* and a fossil high roller—that is, until it was highly doubted she ever walked on that leg. Guess no *Dancing with the Stars*, may be next season?

The speculation is that Lucy is an ancestor no matter how far-flung and wide reaching. Why can't Lucy just be an extinct example of an ancient chimpanzee? And it appears by many accounts that's what she was. The bones are wrong for a human, the shoulder socket is very wrong, the legs are wrong, the hips are wrong, and fibula are wrong. Why don't they call it an extinct chimp or gorilla? Well, because it's not that interesting that's why. Lucy would be just a semi-interesting exhibit at the local museum.

Lucy's pelvis could not pass a human child because it is not wide enough to pass the head of a human infant. But because of her pelvic size, she could pass a chimp. So was Lucy just a chimp or gorilla. Common sense and probability say most likely an extinct chimp. But it should be remembered that the reconstruction has no feet. Ah, but the artwork always displays a human foot on Lucy. Isn't this just a lie to help the evolutionist prove their point? The reality is, if you must lie to prove your point, the value of your point is actually pointless.

The theory as it relates to us automatically uses the assumption that all primates are related somehow. Anthropologists even site the fact all primates have hair and fingerprints. Bad news, all mammals have hair, and even bears can be identified by their own distinctly identifiable paw print. What is the reality here? Even with parts missing, the missing parts are replaced with parts that support evolutionary theory, all this despite finding similar creatures that show no such adaptations whatsoever. Let us be clear here. That is what is commonly known as a lie.

Despite having shoulder blades well adapted to swinging in trees, shoulder sockets pointing up and with a crushed pelvis, Lucy poses more questions than answers. On the hair issue, with the exception of adult dolphins, all mammals have a protective coating of hair before birth. Adult dolphins do not have hair as hair would cause a reduction in its efficiency so it is not needed. It should be noted that while dolphins have almost no hair, they do have hair follicles (mammals, remember).

Humans have 206 bones, but babies have 300; those bones begin to fuse together until adolescence, and this continues until they get to adulthood. It is often stated that humans and chimpanzees share 99 percent the same DNA. It isn't simple task to find out for sure. The nature and structure of genes repeats, but a better estimate is somewhere from 85 percent to 95 percent. The genetic difference of even 2 percent is a pretty far chasm to cross but speculation, supposition, and evolutionary quackery always drives them to even more grandiose claims.

Dolphins have a difference of two chromosomes less from us and how different are they from humans. This isn't speculation that only 2 percent DNA is a lot. For example, we have about 50 percent the same DNA as a banana, and yet people do not use this to say we are related. But a better way of looking at it is, all living things have DNA even viruses, although it is argued viruses are not alive. Potatoes like chimps have forty-eight chromosomes, but the relationship to each other is nonexistent.

Apes, chimps, and orangutans have thirteen ribs on each side for a total of twenty-six arranged in pairs; each side has a match on the other side. Humans have twenty-four ribs, twelve on each side; one less on each side than our supposed cousins. Did evolution or GOD take that rib from us? Interesting question, but if evolution changed us, why lose a rib? There are no signs that we lost one or it just shriveled away, it's just not there. To date, no protohumans have been found with twelve ribs. This is for obvious reasons they don't really exist.

When we look at the difference, we see drastic differences in comparison. Let's start from the top. The brains the great apes are pretty dumb, not being mean here, but the cranial capacity is just not there. The arrangement of the skull does not give much room for improvement. With a heavy brow ridge that slopes backwards, there isn't much room for a large brain.

The jawbone is U-shaped, and their teeth are quite large and heavy to support a mouth adapted solely for chewing vegetation. The difference from humans is recognizable immediately, so Australopithecus cannot be confused with humans. They are just too different. Shoulder sockets face upward in the great apes, good for climbing and swinging in trees. Human shoulder sockets face down. While we do swing our arms, it is for balance while walking, not swinging in trees. The great apes, when they do walk, hold their arms out fully extended, using their arms like a tight rope walker uses a pole. This is a kind of weight-balancing act, shifting with outstretched arm to counteract the effects of gravity and the constant shifting of body mass not adapted for walking.

The ribs in the great apes are greater in number and slope downward like a honeybee hive. Human rib cages are shaped like a barrel. The bones in the great apes are generally smaller even in large creatures because their muscles are thick and dense; this adaptation is better for protecting the vital organs and bones. This is not so in humans. We have larger bones and smaller muscles.

The sacrum in humans has six sacral bones; in the great apes, they have four. The hole in the pelvis is much larger in humans to pass the large head of a human child. Neither apes nor Australopithecus could pass a human child; the birth canal is just too small. No fossils of an anthropoid have ever been found with a pelvis large enough to pass a human child. They have never found a specimen showing the gradual widening of the birth canal as you might expect. Any specimen showing an expected anticipated physical skeletal structure change should be easy to find and litter the floor of every museum in the world, but they apparently don't exist.

The great apes have weak legs and strong arms for climbing. Humans have strong legs for walking and much weaker arms in comparison. The limbs in the great apes are longer in proportion to the body than in humans. The great apes have hands and hands. Humans have hands and feet, and we are remarkably well adapted for walking. Apes, orangutans, and chimps have almost no butt, an absolute necessity for walking upright for long distances. The support of the butt is a necessity to keep the spine from compressing the lower vertebrae. When compared to great apes, one might think the structures are similar. But the truth is much more complex. Out of the three great apes, their DNA is much larger than ours and of course, breeding to a viable offspring is impossible. This is true, and it cannot be demonstrated now or in the past, as fossil evidence in this regard isn't just scanty. It is nonexistent.

The larger DNA in chimps will not combine with us. Ours it's just too small. In addition, receptor sites must line up, which they won't. This is for the simplest of reasons we are not genetically compatible and never were. There are those who would like to say that there are four great apes and would like to include us in that mixture, but it is a loosely concocted theory compounded with no proof. Some anthropologists would like to put us in that mix, but for obvious reasons, we are that remarkably and unmistakably different.

We should consider that there are two separate species of chimpanzees, and they will not interbreed on their own. This is because they are not the same species. Their habits are different; even the mating habits are different. The rule applies that if separated too long, species will diverge into a class that cannot interbreed with each other anymore. Genetic bottlenecking changes the genetic structures and environmental changes for thousands of years so that crossbreeding is not possible.

It was once thought that there were several species of man. No so. To date, all humans can interbreed, a classical requirement for being the same species. Bonobo chimp hybrids have been successfully interbred in captivity, but they cannot be considered a new species. This is because they are not. That species never existed in nature or anywhere else because they are sterile like the mule. This rule speaks the loudest against evolution because for evolution to take place, adaptations like this are critical to the theory but stopped by genetic sterilization to prevent any such change. You will not find evolutionists talking about this point because it scientifically speaks against evolutionary theory.

Prolonged interbreeding leads to sterility and extinction, and if left apart for too long from his species, breeding to a successful viable offspring that can reproduce isn't very probable. As you can see, the genetic influence of change is a slippery slope a careful balancing act that makes genetic change difficult to the point of even extinction. If you are waiting for hybrids to stop the extinction of a species, forget it. Evolutionists leave out a lot of information and allow ignorance to prove their new pseudoscience's point of view. Sterile animals are prevented from procreating because their genetic code will not allow it, and so it would seem it is a virtual genetic dead end that kills the violator's progeny, for the ability to reproduce is stopped forever.

Consider this, species of wolves can crossbreed with dogs because they both separated some 27,000 to 40,000 thousand years ago according to the experts. Modern dogs prove through DNA they are very closely related to the European wolf. This conclusion is fact because they have found fossils and bones of European wolves that prove the genetic links. We can argue about the time line, but all dogs can interbreed; a classic example for being the same species.

Human fossils, next to baboon fossils, next to chimp fossils sounds like a jig saw puzzle. Yeah, I know it doesn't sound very plausible. Throw a gorilla in there and now you're cooking. What kind of puzzle could you make from all that? Speculation starts with the finding of new fossil discoveries. It is assumed all fossils that are located in the same area belong to the same individual but miles apart, apparently, are still acceptable to those who want to believe in the hogwash of evolution.

So let's get this straight. According to the experts, you could interbreed with a genetically equivalent woman forty thousand years ago and have kids? Answer, yes! Reason, because we are the same species? Answer, yes. Man does not change his genetic structure, neither do animal species for the simplest of reasons there is no proof that such changes have occurred in the fossil record. It should be noted there is no evolutionary science, for it doesn't exist, but what does exist is evolutionary speculation. I like to use the term evolutionary guess because it is easier to understand and sounds more like the craps shoot. It really is.

As it was stated earlier, the same species will diverge into different species if they are separated for too long. Really! Genetics, who knew? Evolution is mostly a lie. How long is too long? The answer, it would seem, would be eighty thousand years or a hundred thousand years. How about two hundred thousand years? Some say two million. That is how old they say man is, and sometimes, a million years old. If that is true, then genetic Eve could have babies with Fred Smith up the street, but bonobos and chimps can't have a viable offspring? Answer, yes. Why? Genetic decoding prevents it! While breaking new ground for a new fossil find, remember this there is a genetic code they can never break and never will, for it is too complex for even them to understand.

As in bonobos and chimps, they were either never related or if they were through a common ancestor, they have been separated for a minimum of forty thousand years, too long to propagate the new species, and these are the numbers provided by the evolutionist. Both live on the same continent but don't breed with each other. This is not a case of strange bedfellows but no bedfellows. Science makes a separation based on the ability to reproduce. All humans everywhere can reproduce, making us all the same species. But two almost identical creatures bonobos and chimps cannot interbreed? This should either make or break the evolution theory playbook. The most successful species in the history of the world is reading this book right now!

Based on this the question, how could all 7.4 billion people on the earth be a part of the same species? Remember the interbreeding question, how long can that go on? Science could answer that question, but do they want to? Remember, separation leads to genetic variation and new blood leads to new life. The origins of humans are clouded with mystery by our evolutionary die-hard friends simply because they choose to believe something else clouded in mystery. Essentially, they supply the questions and are very short on any answers. If questioned in depth, they simply try to get you to believe you cannot comprehend the answer because you are not enlightened like they are. The real truth is, one man's enlightenment is another man's delusion.

We are all recipients of that genetic variation. It appears there are rules, and they must be followed, or sterility and extinction occur. This is a fact ignored by our evolutionary friends. Because inbreeding leads to a dead end, and evolution by definition speaks to the conclusion inbreeding has no part on man's march through time. But the truth is, inbreeding might make it possible to help find a deformed skull of a so-called evolutionary cousin. If this is true and science says that it is, how did Eve get her offspring around this insurmountable problem?

Evolution cannot answer this question because they are blinded by the truth. Natural selection and genetic disposition as seen in everyday life tell us Eve and her children would have ended in the fourth or fifth generation, or we would have been a race of drooling cretins, just an easy meal for the local predators and extinct. Evolutionists cannot answer this question because they refuse to believe in a GOD who created the entire universe and also created the DNA in an eternal human species. Long on questions but short on answers; evolutionary speculation, who knew?

Several investigators, including Richard Leakey, have now concluded that two or perhaps three species have been wrongly combined in "Lucy." She was not a human ancestor. At best, she was a form of extinct ape; at worst, she was a mosaic, yet she is still touted as the best "evidence" for human evolution. (Source: John D. Morris, PhD)

According to Ellie Zolfagharifard for the Daily Mail 10 on April 2015 and updated 16 April 2015, when Lucy was put back together, it was found she had a baboon's vertebrae in the mix of Lucy's fossil record. It was noticed because it was just too small to have been a part of the rest of the find.

Gary Sawyer and Mike Smith at the American Museum of Natural History in New York embarked on the reconstruction of Lucy's skeleton. When complete, it was an astounding representation of her kind complete with a human foot, arch and all, and all put together from a single toe.

If we are to believe the missing but fantasied feet proved anything, it was a pure concoction, wishful thinking, and entirely conjecture. Lucy has no feet, and the feet from other Australopithecus tell a very different story than the fraud of Lucy. Australopithecus's feet are very similar to chimp's feet. While rock-hard fact points out fossils are indeed just rock, any depiction of Lucy with feet is a downright hoax.

If Lucy had human feet, she would have been a veritable cripple. She would not have been able to compete with others of her kind that didn't have a human arched foot. The rest of her anatomy leads to an explicit answer, no human feet! Lucy had the chimp foot necessary for her to survive in her chimp world. Fake is the undeniable fact "no human feet on a chimp." If I showed you a picture of a human with horse hooves, you would know it as the fraud it was. But for the experts, apparently, a walking Lucy with human feet causes no alarm at all, but it is still a grandiose fraud. In their exhausting excavation of endless mounds of earth, they have apparently inserted fake feet on an upright walking Lucy that never was.

Remember, if Lucy could read the newspaper hanging upside down by one foot while munching on tree roots with her other foot, she wasn't a human or anything near human, protohuman, or a truck driver named Bernice from Toledo, Ohio. It was discovered that the fossil of a gelada baboon thoracic vertebra was the culprit and somehow had been mixed up with Lucy's remains. Even the experts are throwing out bits and pieces of the old girl. How much of that 40 percent just doesn't belong there in the first place?

> Since it was not attached to any other bones, this possibility should have been weighed. (Source: ice. org) In an interview with CBC radio, lead author Carol Ward said, "Lucy's foot would have been just like yours or mine." But this blatantly ignores prior finds showing that Lucy's foot was actually configured like a hand, with a thumb-like big toe projecting sideways. And what if the foot bone in question was actually from a human and not from an Australopith at all? Since it was not attached to any other bones, this possibility should have been weighed. (Source: "Lucy's New Foot Bone Is Actually Human" by Brian Thomas, MS)

Lucy is an Australopithecus because she has been compared to other known creatures that had their feet-hand thingy present. This demonstrates how, even if she did have feet, they would need to be thrown out because other members of her family had hands for feet. Consider this, a human foot on a chimp would be entirely out of line with the rest of her body structure, which was apparently just an extinct form of chimp.

Why would GOD, nature or evolution, choose to change only the feet? She had the sacral bones of a chimp, two sets of thirteen ribs, shoulder blades of a tree-climbing chimp, a pelvis not suited for human locomotion, and hands adapted for knuckle walking. Sorry, kids, I smell a chimp. Oh, let's not forget, the shoulder sockets facing up. Sad but true, Lucy is an extinct chimp, plain and simple, and without human feet and certainly no human legs to stand on them.

Even some of the experts come short of a positive identification because it is difficult to imagine any creature that was able to change only its feet. Lucy's shoulder sockets are facing upward; this is a prime example of how the great apes' body mechanics are very well adapted for climbing trees. All the great apes, chimps, and orangutans have their shoulders socket facing upward, humans facing down! Sorry, Lucy, you are just a chimp. Hand her a banana and send her back to her fraudulent exhibit. And by the way, the human race called, and we want our feet back.

Lucy is given as the best example of an Australopithecus afarensis; her feet are absent, but other specimens where feet are present, they don't look like human feet at all because they are not. The reconstruction has her looking more like a human that an extinct chimp. But if they portrayed her hanging in a tree, you wouldn't look at her as long as if she is walking on human feet. No wonderment there! But obviously still an elaborate fraud.

> Is one bone singled out from a scrap heap of "greater than 370" individual bones the best evidence for an upright-walking ape?2 If this bone actually was from a "Lucy," it would be the first A. afarensis skeletal feature discovered that is not ideally suited for life in trees. But to assert that this one bone was an Australopith's is to beg the

question. It no more belonged to a Lucy than the famous pig's tooth belonged to the fraudulent "Nebraska Man." This bone has not proven that Lucy walked, but instead illustrates how improper science leads to flawed conclusions. (Source: "Lucy's New Foot Bone Is Actually Human" by Brian Thomas, MS. http://www.icr.org/article/lucys-new-foot-bone-actually-human/)

If she was portrayed hanging upside down from a tree limb, you would wonder why she wasn't in the zoo! The fact remains a walking Lucy may have balanced on a tree trunk crossing a river, but she didn't do it for long her body structure bears out this irrefutable fact. In humans, shoulder sockets face downward. This critical adaptation is simply because humans don't travel by swinging in trees the great apes do.

Humans must have shoulder sockets facing down because while we walk with our legs, we balance ourselves with our arms. As a matter of fact, none of the primates have this adaptation with the special exception of one "human" but as outlined here, we are not related to chimps by any stretch of the imagination with the exception of diluted evolutionists. Remember, we have huge brains, weak arms and legs that can outdistance even the horse. Most anthropologists would have you believe we lost that socket somewhere in the past. Where is it in the fossil record to prove it? You can ask the question and the answer will be well, er...ah...we haven't found it yet. The simple truth is this, if they did find an adapted shoulder socket by itself, the scientific conclusion would inevitably be classified as human in origin.

To date, that creature has not been found. But after 156 years, they are still looking. The adaptation of the foot, shoulder, and knee are an important one because it demonstrates human or not. The shoulder joint faces up takes the stress off the joint so the primate can hang from trees. For humans, the stress is considerable, and the force of body weight makes it difficult for us to hang by anything for very long. The angle is just wrong. It stresses the socket until the pain is unbearable and you drop.

Our great ape friends can do it as long as the muscle will hold out, not the weak bad angel socket like us humans. Remember, we are Homo sapiens; shoulder sockets are downward, not upward like our primate friends. While some science will stress the similarity of the two species (humans and the great apes), there are drastic differences. There are radical and distinct differences. Remember, the apes have their legs where their arms should be, and so upper body strength is massive compared to us with puny humans.

The science of finding and identifying man's "prehistoric ancestors" runs in a predictable pattern. A press conference is announced and the discovery of an ape-like "ancestor" revealed with an artist's impression of what the creature looks like, and the discoverer becomes famous, earning money on lecture tours. The actual fossil bones are scanty and the imagination runs wild.

Later, when more evidence is found, the "ancestor" turns out to be totally human or totally ape. The Neanderthal man is an example of one find that turns out to be totally human. Once this find is removed as an intermediate form, you can expect another great discovery to save the day. The latest discovery is "Lucy." (Source: forerunner.com. "Lucy Fails Test as Missing Link" article by editorial staff. December 22, 2007)

The extent of accumulated genetic difference enabled the researchers to speculate about when the different populations separated. They estimate that bonobos, which live south of the Congo River, split off from the ancestors of modern chimpanzees about 800,000 years ago. Western chimps appear to have separated from central and eastern chimpanzees about 500,000 years ago, and central and eastern chimps divided about 250,000 years ago. (Source: Science Daily article dated April 22, 2007)

This source continues that the three chimp species are genetically more different than any two humans on the planet in comparison. Imagine that the truth of evolution is, has, and always been a fraud. Those chimps apparently monkeyed around more than is humanly possible. They were apparently the same species; at one time, great-great-uncle Australopithecus? It would seem so!

The largest study to date of genetic variation among chimpanzees has found that the traditional, geography-based sorting of chimps into three populations—western, central, and eastern—is underpinned by significant genetic differences, two to three times greater than the variation between the most different human populations. (Source: Science Daily. April 22, 2007)

What does the evidence point to? Well, the obvious conclusion we can find in Wikipedia. They conclude that Australopithecus and bonobos are ancestors because the bone structures are very similar. But by comparison of either creature to humans is just not there. If this is true, Lucy is an extinct bonobos (a pygmy chimp).

According to one scholar, A. Zihlman, Australopithecus's body proportions closely resemble those of bonobos pan (paniscus), leading evolutionary biologists such as Jeremy Griffith to suggest that bonobos may be phenotypically similar to Australopithecus. (Source: Wikipedia, Australopithecus)

What is the conclusion here? Australopithecus is more closely related to the Pan bonobos than bonobos are related to us, our supposed closest living relative. Australopithecus was, is and, always has been a chimp. It doesn't matter what the artwork shows. She is just a chimp. Lucy was just a bonobo, not extinct just ask her great-great-grand-children the pygmy chimp "bonobos."

At this point, the evolutionist is standing on the four corners of a square block with critical corners breaking off. It is easily seen that that old book of biblical fairy tales makes more sense than our ancient ancestor's evolutionary change one body part at a time… ridiculous!

Evolutionary science has rules—strict rules—but the one they cannot refute is the absence of transitional forms turning from ape to human. They just don't exist, for if they did, surely someone would have mentioned it by now.

You are a human and according to the fossil record, you have always been a human. You have the ability to choose what you want to believe. But the truth doesn't care what you believe, the truth is the truth. It is a matter of faith versus speculation, but remember, this faith will lead you to the truth, and speculation is never truth at best, just a wild guess.

Chapter 4

○

Transitional Fossils?

If you would like to believe in the evolutionary process, then consider this. At the time of the writing of this book, evolutionists have not found one transitional fossil. Let's be clear here, if we evolved from one species to another, then paleontologists should be able to provide an animal that shows signs of transitioning from one species to another. The evolutionist short-circuits this logic with because the great apes resemble us, any fossil found of the big three (apes, chimps, and the orangutan) are obviously our ancestors.

This nonfact is eluded by evolutionists; they never attempt to resolve this critical but important anticipated change. Changes that are anticipated are not found in the fossil record at all. This is because they cannot provide one transitional shoulder joint or hip, or even the Holy Grail, a human foot on an evolving chimp.

Fossils don't provide even one example of any creature ever found anywhere that shows signs of transitioning from one species to another species. What? Not even one? The answer is pretty clear—no, not one. If it was so and nature will not change a successful species, the transitional phase would not be found in the fossil record. Remarkably, it isn't found and creates a great chasm in the evolutionary community that they prefer not to talk about. This absence is at the core of why evolution is not a science, no validation and absolutely no proof.

For any transitional species to occur, they must have been successful. In other words, the one species that has changed must be more successful than the one it replaced. Why would it change if it could not effectively outnumber the creature it replaced? Where are all the bones to prove this critical point of view? The answer is pretty clear here. They don't exist. Is it more difficult to believe that the constant change through millennia would produce numbers that were nearly impossible to find a million years later? Or could we surmise that the change found is only a transition from Australopithecus to chimpanzee?

When we consider the extreme conservation provided by the fossil record, this would account for the two creatures still recognizable as ancestors today. When we consider that the chimpanzee and bonobos cannot interbreed to a viable reproducible copy because of a time separation, could it be that Australopithecus was a result of the union of the two species when they could interbreed? Even more complex would be Australopithecus was the great-granddaddy of them both. The experts will say foolishness, but the thinking man will conclude it is not only plausible but more than probable.

If you consider that the circumstances should fit the facts, then the theory I have provided makes perfect sense. It accounts for the dilemma provided by the fossil record; however, it also provides for a genetic time clock that is so slow the entertainment provided by evolutionary theory is lost?

We are not talking about protohumans alone; there are no, none, nada transitional fossils of any creature that ever lived changing from one species to another one. If they ever existed, they would be found and if they found even so much as a mollusk, you would know about it because it would be on every news channel in the world. Consider this, seashells found on Mount Everest is still identified with living ancestors found today. It would seem the seashells achieved genetic equilibrium when the peaks of Everest were on the bottom of the ocean floor. Apparently, evolutionists change things. GOD does not!

Believing the lie is difficult to do with wishful thinking, fantasy or artwork depicting such miraculous finds. But the truth is even more scientific than you would believe. If man were the only species to change into something else, clearly, we would be the only one ever. According to the theory of evolution, creatures change for survival, and natural selection should play a critical role. The differences between the chimp and your brother-in-law are so great no evolutionist can begin to explain what disaster—natural or otherwise—could possibly begin to explain why a chimp would change into a man.

If the evolutionary theory says anything, it states that evolution is a slow process taking hundreds of thousands of years. The evolutionary process makes improvements gradually and occasionally through mutation. If man underwent change through some special circumstances—environment, chemical or as simply as the biological need for survival—this would affect other creatures also. But those creatures also did not change. These changes are not found in the fossil record at all.

It is a scientific fact that no mutation has ever led to an improvement in any species ever. A mutated gene is not a good thing and can lead to deformations, disease, and finally, death. Cancer is the direct result of mutated genes. But for a seashell to decide it wanted to win the Boston Marathon millennia later is no more ridiculous than a chimp deciding climbing for bananas is no fun, so let's become human with feet to walk to the store instead. The truth is, no explanation is ever given as to why chimps would want to be human.

Once, I was asked by a supervisor who wanted to promote me to a higher position why didn't I want to be like him? When I refused his offer, he looked puzzled and asked why not. My answer was, why would I want to be like you, you're divorced and haven't seen your kids in three months, no thanks! Is the truth evolutionists deluded themselves with such logic? Of course, chimps are an example of early humans that wanted to be so much like us that now here we are is just silly!

This is demonstrated in the simple frog, which can have his DNA altered by a parasite. When attacked by the parasite, the frog grows three legs, making it a cripple. This in turn makes it an easy meal for the crane. The cycle repeats itself, when the crane's droppings find water; the flatworm infested droppings repeat the cycle, as it starts all over again. The only beneficiary of this recurring cycle being the crane and the parasite, the frog ends up on the menu. If you google three-legged frog, the Chinese consider it lucky and have used it as a good luck charm for hundreds of years. The three-legged frog is certainly lucky for the Chinese, but invariably unlucky for the poor frog.

The genetic code is so precise it will kill, cripple, or sterilize any creature to prevent the spread of mutations, or genetic incompatibility. This could be best described as a genetic doomsday bomb in place to prevent any genetic change, apparently in spite of evolutionary thought or theory. Yes, you got it straight; the envisioned evolutionary change is the death nail to any creature in a mutated gene pool.

If any creature had its chromosomes altered, it would be a dead end, unless it could not find a suitable mate with the same genetic alteration at the same genetic position. These chances must be in the billions. Evolutionists, we get it. It just happens so slow, and gradual differences are minute. If the study of evolution teaches anything, it teaches species resist change even for millions of years. This is the irrefutable fact they dismiss with wishful thinking and art.

Natural selection can accommodate and, at the same time, confuse the issue. If large brains became an issue for survival, wouldn't some of our competitors have developed large brains also? None of our competitors demonstrate any such change. A fossilized lion, baboon, or hyena would clearly demonstrate no significant cranial improvement. And so, any size difference would be attributed to age and size of the individual subject alone.

Natural adaptations like speed, strength, and stamina are found throughout in the natural world. Because it works, the same speed required to kill an antelope by the lion deprives him of a meal if the antelope is just a little faster. Who or what drove us to be intelligent? Where in the bone pile were the challenges that drove our enlarged brain development? This is truly natural selection, a requirement for the prize of survival. A good example would be the badger or the wolverine smaller than us certainly, but you better never try to pet one; they will kill you.

As with the Australopithecus and the bonobos chimp, even after two million years of supposed evolutionary change, the two are still recognized as related. So, in two million years of natural selection, two species are still recognized as very similar, but during this process, one of those special creatures evolved into us. The problem starts to become glaring when you realize what natural process would cause the change in only one of the dozens of creatures surviving in the same continent at the same time. The answer is clear, it didn't happen.

The genetic time bomb is so precise it is imbedded in the genetic code of every living creature past, present, and future. In the end, for the evolutionist, it is simply a case of undying solid as a rock faith. Yes, I said it, and it's true. As a matter of fact, I would imagine the faith required to compel someone to contradict the obvious must be unshakeable.

Let's see if we can come up with some questions for our evolutionary die-hard friends.

1. Did shoulder sockets turn downward gradually or all at once?
2. Did our hominid ancestors lose the extra set of ribs gradually or all at once?
3. Did our hominid ancestors switch legs to arms and arms to legs gradually or all at once?
4. Has there ever been a hominid found with five sacral bones? We have; six chimps have four.
5. Has there ever been any hominid found with twelve ribs? (Present man excluded)
6. What is the best example of any hominid with an arched foot with the big toe pointing forward? (Humans exempt, of course)
7. Has there ever been any hominid found that can be used as proof to answer any of the above questions? No, I didn't think so.
8. Did Australopithecus have a baculum and did the females have a baubellum?
9. Where are the fossils that will answer just one of the above questions?

More on number eight, chimps and gorillas have a penis bone called a baculum; in females, it is a clitoris bone called a baubellum. While not present in modern humans, these bones still exist in chimps and gorillas. Research by myself is truly inconclusive as to if Australopithecus had one, but due to the similarities with chimps, they undoubtedly did. Apparently, the Australopithecus fossil record is so poor even scientists cannot provide a single baubellum or baculum.

This leads to an interesting question, if we are related to the chimp, when did we lose the penis bone? Another interesting inquiry would be because of its prevalence in mammals is quite common, but apparently missing in the orangutan. The absence of the baculum in the orangutans and the evolutionary exclusion of orangutan as our ancestors make one wonder; the reproductive organs of the orangutan are more closely related to humans than chimps.

Why do the evolutionists try to pound this square peg into a round hole with the assertion our closest living relative is the chimp? The answer it appears is because chimps live in community of close-knit family units. The male orangutan only appears to breed and leaves his beloved knocked up and alone. If Australopithecus had one (baculum) and so do chimps, that is a pretty severe adaptation to take place and should be found in the fossil record somewhere, which it is not.

In a world where we have dominated the planet, messing around with one's sex organs doesn't sound like a good idea. But to the evolutionists, the question goes ignored, because they don't know. When claiming to be an expert, the evolutionists don't like questions they can't answer. To be more specific, even a single bone can pose an unanswerable question for the experts. It is always an embarrassment for an evolutionist to say I don't know. This, for obvious reasons, especially if they don't know, it is embarrassing for any expert to be ignorant. What else don't they know? It is safe to say the evolutionists have evolved to a new species. Let's call them ego-lutionists.

If absence of proof is anything, it is proof of absence. There are no fossils that can answer any of the questions above because they don't exist. The answer seems to point to an ancient hominid freak show where all the questions above were answered overnight. As stated earlier, mating with relatives is bad for business. Diversity is the rule. If an extinct hominid was successful, his remains will out-number the creature he replaced. Where are they? The only logical explanation that could possibly make sense is because they haven't found them yet. This is the only logical explanation! Where are all the fossils and who could be hiding them? What about the rule that a successful species will not change? Where are our transitional kin? The answer seems to be—they don't exist. A dog knows if you can't find the toy, there isn't any toy to be found.

Australopithecus are only found in small numbers because they existed like the chimp in small numbers. Finding so few could easily explain the whole story. Australopithecus bred himself to extinction or he found a way out via the chimp and bonobos. They are still rec-ognized as bonobos because their skeletal differences were a result of continued inbreeding and the genetic results of it. Australopithecus met their end while the chimp survives. They will exclaim that cra-nial differences in Australopithecus and the bonobos are glaring but can easily be explained through interbreeding; one of the major developments provided by incest, a deformed skull.

There is something to be gained here; unlike the bonobos and the chimp isolation from each other can divide them forever, espe-cially if that separation is for too long, forty thousand years. Now consider this separation in the human species, it has provided our kind with genetic diversity in our species, and inbreeding as a prob-lem can be avoided, and so this is no longer a problem. Separation is a plus in the human species. Where did we get that special adap-tation from? Remember, all humans are genetically compatible and can produce a viable human child. Who devised this awesome plan? Was it GOD?

Be fruitful and multiply. Whereas the chimp has a time stamp on his DNA, no apparent time limit exist on us humans simply because our habits avoid this through sheer numbers. Could it be true that no human is separated by any other human by less than forty thousand years? Given this example, how about thirty thousand years or twenty thousand years, or GOD forbid, six thousand years.

Now we can see that even in the lie, there is some truth, but you need to find it because they will not give it to you easily.

In a world where lions, tigers, and bears roamed the earth, coming out of the trees didn't seem like a good idea. This question is easily answered because it didn't happen. In a world where nasty flesh-eating creatures roamed the earth, there appeared man, not a chimp with a psychotic drive to kill lions for giggles and grins. Homo sapiens (us), a creature driven to kill animals with the strength ten times his own. Man armed only with his drive for survival and not just for himself, but more importantly, for the survival of his own kind. Why? You may ask. Because the GOD of creation put it there, and now you know and that is why. With danger came faith and the desire for a safer world and the belief I am not afraid my GOD protects me against even the lion.

This drive was instilled in him because he had no other choice. Kill or be killed. This was serious business. If it is faster, be smarter; if it is stronger, be smarter still; and if it eats your young, you will hunt it until it is a problem no more. That's the man I see—defiant, determined, and deadly—not a bonobos chimp with a bad hair day. But this frail, naked, and outnumbered species had a big edge. This edge was and is so powerful the evolutionists could never imagine what it was.

Out of all earth's creatures, the one least physically adapted for the wild in which he found himself, man killed his predators all the way to the top of the food chain! Equipped with the most powerful killing tool ever available anywhere, the human brain. Equipped with the tools of man's trade—spears, clubs, and snares, hunting parties, and killing pits—do chimps do things like that? Of course, they don't. But from with the command from GOD, that gave us reason to fight, "be fruitful and multiply," and we did!

What was the edge? What kept very vulnerable human children alive until their adolescence? Their GOD! He gave mankind a reason to hope, a reason to believe. This gave man the belief he could master not only the vastness of the arboreal planes that he found himself in, but also the courage needed for the task at hand. Yes, the faith in something greater than himself—his GOD.

Armed with the power of his GOD, this gave man the courage he needed for this desperate, naked, and ill-fitted creature to conquer the world in which he lived. Man conquered all he surveyed, all of this in the wilds of the primitive jungle, to not just survive but to thrive. How arduous was this task you might ask? It was unimaginable to us modern-day humans.

How puny are we anyway? The lion has the strength of ten men. The cheetah can reach speeds of seventy miles per hour. The chimp can pull us apart with its bare hands. Baboons have been known to kill even the cheetah. Given the above facts and archaeological evidence, the baboon was our fiercest competitor.

A *New York Times* article dated June 23, 1981, written by Bayard Webster details the slaughter of ninety giant extinct baboons. Their average weight was 140 pounds, and the task was not for the faint of heart. I won't belabor the gory details, but the only reference given the killers was a hominid. (Source: nytimes.com)

It should be remembered the find apparently did not yield any of the hominid fossils you might expect. But the weapons used in the ensuing battles were found—the stone ax. Neanderthal is a possibility. Homo sapiens are a more likely suspect. But stone axes are never attributed to Australopithecus, and chimps don't use them either. Evolution is widely accepted as the truth by a scant few, but it is far from providing scientific facts. In truth, it is not based on scientific evidence at all. This is because it cannot be measured by the scientific method.

The results are not measurable or predictive, and certainly, not reproducible. Lucy is gone, and she isn't coming back. Java man, Nebraska man, Piltdown man, they have all gone to the trash heap of a patch work of repair after repair to the evolutionary theory. We find that with improvements made in genetic study that the gap between chimps and humans widens with every new discovery.

Has this new endeavor provided a closer walk with the chimpanzee? Previous studies of human and chimpanzee DNA indicate a 98–99% match of identical DNA. These studies have focused on a narrow area of the total genome—the gene coding regions. This is a very limited area and a tiny fraction of the roughly 3 billion DNA base pairs that comprise our genetic blueprint. Recent studies have shown that the amount of DNA difference is not 1–2%, but more like 4%. This is at least double the percentage difference claimed by scientists for years. (Source: http://www.creation-studies.org/Education/isevolution science.html)

So close and yet so far away, the 2 percent touted as the difference between chimps and humans is now 4 percent. The better science gets, the farther away our supposed ancestors get from us. Remember, the dolphins at 2 percent, how different from us are they?

Darwinism prediction of rampant, albeit gradual, change affecting all lineages through time is refuted. The record is there, and the record speaks for tremendous anatomical conservation. Change in the manner Darwin expected is just not found in the fossil record. (Source: Niles Eldredge, PhD)

Not found in the fossil record? Doctor Eldredge has hit the nail on the head. If there is proof of the existence for a transitional form of anything, where is it? Is it still out there, and we haven't found it yet? Perhaps if the transitional form of hominid were found first, it would be a simple foregone conclusion, and we wouldn't be mystified with the theory anymore.

The extreme rarity of transitional forms in the fossil record persist as a trade secret of Paleontology. Evolutionary trees that adorn our textbooks have data only at the tips and nodes of their branches; the rest is inference, however reasonable, not in the evidence of fossils. (Source: Stephen Jay Gould, PhD)

What? This is known as the trade secrets of paleontology. I guess it's not a secret any longer. What else are they keeping secret? Again, the absence of proof is absolutely proof of absence. A child knows if you can't find it, it just isn't there!

> But as by this theory innumerable transitional forms must have existed, why do we not find them embedded in the countless numbers in the crust of the earth? The case at present must remain inexplicable and may be truly argued as a valid argument against the views here entertained. (Source: Charles Darwin)

Mr. Darwin was obviously a genius because he knew and understood the dilemma in trying to prove his new theory. He understood the missing pieces and was consoled by the fact intermediate transitional species would be found later on. One hundred and fifty-six years later and they are still looking. Mr. Darwin provided the criteria to end the experiment and explained it this way.

> If it could be demonstrated that any complex organ existed which could not possibly have been formed by numerous, successive, slight modification, then my theory would absolutely break down. (Source: Charles Darwin)

It has broken down; Australopithecus is and always has been an extinct chimp. It has been noted they are very close to bonobo chimps. If this is true, then Australopithecus are no more like us than the bonobos are. This is a major setback for the evolutionists, because a two-million-year-old ancestor of a chimp points to the origin of chimps, not of man. The fossil record points to the fact Australopithecus is not extinct, but alive and well in their offspring—the pygmy chimp.

Further explanation is not needed to let us theorize if a two-million-year-old creature is recognizable today. How little has it changed after two million years? Conclusion, not very much, so this points to very, very, slow change at least for the chimps. As stated earlier, you can't date a rock or tell how long it has been a rock; arguing dates is silly because times and dates are erroneous because there is no test to rely on. It is simply a matter of opinion.

It is interesting to note interbreeding between any species leads to abnormalities in the offspring. Any differences between Australopithecus and chimps could be easily explained in this manner. But this explanation is totally ignored by the so-called experts. Interbreeding for generations and natural selection explain the statements above, but if Australopithecus and bonobos could mate to viable offspring, where in the record does that leave us? The answer is obviously in a class all of our own.

Chapter 5

Monkey or Man

It is time to try and bring the subject full circle by exploring the hype and myth with our cousins, the Neanderthals. With a scanty fact thrown in here or there, we come to the crux of the matter, forty-six or forty-eight chromosomes. My bet is on forty-six because interbreeding between the two species is certain. What does science say? Sadly, science has not said very much, folks. It seems they would rather you not know simply because they accept all converts ignorant of the facts or not. Any assertion that we came from chimps is simply just a best guess by the atheist, corrupting a fake science with fake ideas. I would like to point it is an educated guess, but who has done the educating?

Education is relevant but only if it is the truth. Evolution has its drawbacks, and these drawbacks are becoming greater as science catches up with the truth. The controversy began in the United States in July 1925 during what would be known as the Scopes Monkey Trial. This viewpoint has plagued the educational system ever since.

At the Scopes Monkey Trial, Clarence Darrow tried to argue the ape was a distant relative to modern man. William Jennings Bryant argued that the ape was something man could devolve to if left unchecked to revel in his own sin. Who was right? No one will tell you the answer to this question because we are on the verge of asking questions that no one can answer. Fact or fantasy, you decide but despite claims of mental superiority to many questions, they are left as blank pages in the theory of evolution!

What GOD has brought you is science and the truth of it. From the mind of GOD to the hand of man, we have proven ourselves ready and worthy to ask unanswerable questions. We can achieve the miraculous with the greatest creation itself, the majesty of the human mind. Eventually, we will get the answers, but evolution has provided no experiments to prove anything. Shouldn't we just move on to the next experiment? How about the GOD of the universe? The more you learn about creation, the more the creator becomes clear. Life is special and if you take the mantel of science, you should be committed to the truth; if not that, then perhaps a car salesman.

But even as we would limit the minds of others because of our own vanity, it is not the theory of relativity told to children in the third grade so they can have it mastered by the fifth. The majesty of the human mind is in itself sacred and a special gift to us from GOD. For in us man and our delicate and beautiful counterparts woman, we have looked into our own souls and have found the master of it all—GOD!

If any man holds a light no one else can see, he is the saddest of creatures; he has made a fool of himself. Should we fault even the writings of one of the finest minds of his time? I want to thank Charles Darwin; he was definitely a genius, a giant of science with his theory. He made all the sciences better. Zoology, anthropology, paleontology all made better because they were all constructed with a single thought, which is this perfection does exist. It is a sad state of affairs that led evolutionists that equate the new fossil find as proof positive of their ludicrous assertions. The belief that we came from our brother, the chimp, it is not scientific, it cannot be tested, and predictions of outcomes are impossible to prove.

Darwin started an experiment that still goes on today. What he provided was an alternate viewpoint of creation. It has come to its inevitable conclusion; man could not create himself no matter how hard the evolutionists worked at it. Therefore, what is the next experiment? Will it be space aliens or just anyone or anything but GOD? With excerpts from others, we are able to peer into the mind that was the genius of Darwin. What do others say about the man? Let's look and see.

> "Darwin didn't know about human genes, but he was such a good scientist," Berra said, "that he was ahead of his time in linking his finding in plants to his own family." "He was the one who developed this concept of inbreeding depression—a reduction in offspring—and therefore had enough information to begin to wonder about his own marriage and his children's health," Berra said. "The apparent infertility of three of the six surviving Darwin children will remain a mystery," Berra said. But population studies have suggested that statistically, offspring of consanguineous marriages are at higher risk for infertility. "We can't really say they didn't leave offspring because they were the product of a cousin marriage. On the other hand, being the product of cousin marriage does have this infertility component. So one of six, you wouldn't worry. Two, there seems to be a chance this is the reason. Three out of six didn't leave offspring, so that's a fairly strong possibility," Berra said.
> (Source: https://www.sciencedaily.com/relea ses/2010/05/100503111420.htm. May 3, 2010)

Darwin, after all, was a scientist; his motives were purely the quest of knowledge and ultimately the truth. Had he received the information he wanted in the census, perhaps he would have been able to curtail the infant mortality rate of his day. But sadly, the question was never asked of the population. Let's get back to the question, was Moses a scientist? We cannot know how he came to the conclusion that mating with relatives was bad business, but his law was correct thousands of years before Darwin opened his first book.

Mating with relatives leads to death and disease and ultimately extinction. This is the truth, and the truth is GOD. Had it been otherwise, He would have told us so. Moses came to these conclusion millennia before the men and women that continue its practice prove him right to this very day. It is very possible that Moses had firsthand accounts of inbreeding because the pharaohs practiced it. The inevitable outcomes were simply observed by Moses as the truth.

Could the living god of Egypt who refused Moses's demand for freedom ten times was in fact an inbred idiot? One would wonder considering the multiple horrific plagues suffered by himself and his people. The elongated skulls of the pharaohs tell a strange tale that makes one wonder, how closely related were the pharaohs to Neanderthal? When compared to skulls of Neanderthals, the comparison is dramatic and often times startling. But you should know, evolutionists do not study this phenomenon because it just doesn't help evolution or its wildly contentious belief system.

When I say our cousins, Neanderthal, we should look at the genetic probability that if you are Asian, white or even black with white in your heritage, you carry some of the genes of Neanderthal. It is estimated that Europeans are anywhere from 2 to 4 percent Neanderthal in their genetic makeup. Let's remember, 4 percent is a lot in the genetic structure.

This being true that Asians also carry the Neanderthal genetic markers, who exactly were these people—those Neanderthals of common myth? Successful species survive, and the drive to do so is as strong as any human emotion we can find in the vastness of our human dialectic, the quest for the truth and, finally and incredibly, perfection itself. Neanderthal survived. He passed his genome as far as he could, even though it was diluted, because Homo sapiens vastly outnumbered our more beastlike relatives. Science knows this as fact. Science tells us that exchange between the two went one way. Male Neanderthal and female Homo sapiens, we know this because female Neanderthal DNA is not found in any genetic structure in the bloodline of man. The thought is female Neanderthal were sterile when introduced to Homo sapiens DNA. The question to be answered is this, were female Neanderthal, even on the dating list for us, Home sapiens?

Did GOD provide a genetic roadblock to prevent such unions from producing offspring? Could it possibly be that Sally the Neanderthal was just too wild and dangerous to entertain a romantic relationship with? Compelling questions, but there are answers not from scientists but directly from the Bible.

The mating habits of the pharaohs were incestuous—fathers, mothers, daughters, sisters, brothers, and cousins all intermingled with each other. The Neanderthal was on a biological doomsday clock; female Neanderthal died out because either mating with humans produced sterile offspring or mating with humans was not allowed by Neanderthal standards or human. Perhaps the question is simpler than that and provided for in the pages of the Bible. The royalty of ancient Egypt would never intermingle with slaves and let's face it, if you were not in the royal house, you were a slave.

GOD is the truth, and the truth is perfection. If science is the quest for truth, then why do they cringe at GOD's attention to detail? Is it because they see His handiwork even in the fossils record? Everything we are learning about our supposed genetic relatives points to a brutal existence, and even cannibalism was practiced in their small groups. In references to Noah and the description given of the people in his time, they were extremely wicked. As far as social norms go, cannibalism is pretty wicked, and the people that do it are shunned from normal human activity. Let us consider Neanderthal ate each other. How wrong is that?

Science explains that the last Neanderthal died thirty thousand years ago, but this assertion is clouded by the fact that we virtually bred them out of existence. The truth is sometimes obvious, and conclusions can be hard to come by. Let's look at the facts. He was as strong as two or three men, had more brain capacity than any human alive today and was by everyone's reasoning a brute. When deprived of a female Neanderthal mate, he turned his desires to earthly women.

It is difficult to imagine a flesh-eating genius with the strength of two men, but if he truly was able to procreate with modern woman, why would we believe otherwise? Common sense may lead us to this conclusion because we equate intelligence with civility, but that may be flawed thinking when Neanderthal ruled the roost. Consider the genius in some of the most power-hungry people ever to breathe free air.

In their quest for dominance, nothing under GOD great creation was left undone. From the breeding farms in Nazi Germany to the gulags of Soviet Russia, and let's not forget millions starved to death in the Great Chinese Revolution. Neanderthal is alive and well and exerts his dominance in their genetic offspring to this very day. The lessons we have learned are not very many but to discredit the Bible for providing, "Thou shall not kill," is ridiculous. Only a Neanderthal would have a problem with its logic.

The Bible provides as it were, a tale of two cities. GOD's most fantastic creation, man, and the attempt by Satan to pollute man with a creation of his own, Neanderthal. Man, one creation who is seeking the truth, the beauty, and the relevance of man. Neanderthal is and was an egotistical power mad manipulator of the world and every other creation around him. Homo sapiens, meet the Neanderthals. His brain is bigger, "the better to trick you by." He has the strength of two men, although not any more. He still retains the genetic ego of two to three men, and he detests you!

This story is in your Bible. It is in every page if you have the intellect and the clearness of mind to comprehend the truth. These creatures go by many names—Nephilim, Goliath of Gath, Og, and the people who lived in the cities of the Geshurites, Gezrites, and Amalekites and Neanderthal. Atheists tout the killing of these people as proof that GOD kills, violating "Thou shall not kill." The taking down of these cities may have been, in reality, genocidal self-defense. But evolutionists don't examine these facts for simple reasons; it doesn't prove their point (there is no GOD). It seems that the people of Moses's time were terrified of these so-called people (Neanderthal). Could it be for obvious reasons?

The Bible does give leniency for self-defense and giving the idolatry of the time this may have been a kill or be killed issue. The worship of any god should take into account the practices of its worshippers. Given the practices of these ancients, many would consider their abdominal acts a one-way ticket out of the human race. This being true, could it possibly be that GOD was protecting his creation from those that were not really human but an elaborate fake designed to destroy GOD's creation through breeding, murder, and savagery?

While it is certain today, we can provide conclusive proof that many of us carry Neanderthal DNA to this day at about 2 percent. What is not known is what percent our ancestors carried with them three or four thousand years ago. Considerably more! While we may still have some recessive genes that dominate—white skin; blue, green, grey, and hazel eyes. Let's not forget the intelligent manipulator, those who see the people around them as a minor distraction; their end goal is to dominate, manipulate, and to control.

It is safe to say that while our DNA has been washed out to 2 percent thousands of years ago, the Neanderthal DNA should have been much higher of a percent. This point is proven simply by mathematics. The science of genetics should be able to tell us when they really die out, it should be an easy thing to tabulate. But will they ever do it? We have been in opposition to the Neanderthal for millennia. His seed apparently is trapped in us, and we are given the opportunity to accept those genetic traits or oppose them to reveal our true purpose, the pursuit of perfection and truth. All truth is eternal and when you find it, your truth will be eternal.

Neanderthal, by almost every account, was a flesh-eating cannibal. The very act of cannibalism is repugnant to most people and is odd enough to question the practitioner's humanity or lack thereof. Most of the evidence points to the fact they ate each other, but to suggest they would not eat Homo sapiens is far-reaching. If they were smarter, stronger, and you were on the menu, I think we need to look no further as to why they went extinct. We killed them for we had no other choice! By any measure of any society, ancient or otherwise, should you encounter someone eating their own kind to exterminate it would seem like a good idea. To do otherwise would be prerequisite to being eaten.

If my assertion is correct that thousands of years ago man was polluted with Neanderthal DNA, then how could we search for the truth of it? Should we look at the progeny of Neanderthal and see how he has plagued us until this very day? Although many might think this assertion is incorrect, it is interesting to note that criminals of specific crimes share anomalies in the exact location in their DNA. What? Yes, it's true; studies have shown that despite the many differences in people, criminal behavior can be traced back to the makeup of certain DNA strands. Anomalies found in identical genetic position regardless of the race or family background of the criminals being tested.

The real issue may be that while we may have genetic anomalies that may lead us to a life of crime, at the same time, we also have genetic anomalies that dispose us to a different genetic disposition, not to act on the bad influence of those should we say "Neanderthal tendencies." Could it be possible that we control the destiny of our very own DNA? Is it impossible?

Not so fast. It is a proven fact that progeny incorporates knowledge learned from parents, knowledge they could have not known otherwise. Experiments with mice and rats bear this out. Is our DNA the key to our past, present, and future, or do mice and rats talk to one another? Sometimes, even scientific testing can lead to anomalies not easily explainable.

If we look back at human history, we can find that man is a creature that has always found that killing each other just comes naturally. It would be safe to say especially for those plagued with those "Neanderthal tendencies." The drive to kill each other and its root cause can be found in human history. The pages of the Bible are littered with tales of the man in charge manipulating others in a quest for dominance and of course war.

Once, we were able to kill only one person at a time but now millions with the push of a button. How far have we come in the last five thousand years? The answer is sad, not very far unless you consider genocide and mass murder progress. If you have a grin smeared across your face at the thought of mass murder as an improvement of man, perhaps you should be genetically tested. My bet is that you have more Neanderthal genetic makeup than the normal person.

Evolutionist claims that we are now no longer Homo sapiens, but we are now Homo sapiens sapiens is just silly. The name was invented to convey this message, which is this—we have evolved from wise men to wise, wise men and all that since the 1960s. Well really now? How much evil is evil? How evil is 2 to 4 percent? I am not making the assertion that if you have Neanderthal genes, you are evil, but rather those who control those tendencies control their very own DNA to become better, smarter, and in a few words, complete human beings. If we consider ourselves evolved and are so smug about our intelligence, then let us think about how far we have come. Have we evolved to the point that our great claim to fame is Facebook and cell phones? Frankly, I am not impressed with the results.

Is it possible that we see that we have evolved into something new and improved? It is a sad commentary that we haven't come as far as evolutionists would like you to believe. Our ability to function in a complex world as an evolved being is a narcissistic viewpoint at best. The challenges faced by us today pale in comparison to our ancestors of the past. This is a deliberate attempt to show the evolution working in us not demonstrated by man in any age, past or present. It may even be that the evolutionist sees the nonbelief in GOD as a step up the evolutionary ladder. But we will soon see we really haven't come that far.

Biblical history is accurate, and many passages in its pages are verifiable by secondary outside evidence. Should we look at the religious beliefs of our ancestors to measure how far Homo sapiens sapiens has come? If nothing else, as our atheist friends says, seeing is believing.

Chapter 6

Theory or Law

If you can evolve, can you devolve? Apparently, you can. There is a single case of a man in China who only has forty-four chromosomes because two fused together. What does that say about this chance discovery in the human population? It is only a mere one in seven billion. Not very likely! Albeit the odds in this chance happening are extremely rare, the chances of evolving from some protein-laden soup are even much less likely.

If we are not precise in our conclusions, how can our conclusions be precise? It is either the truth or it isn't. Science is not a matter of right and wrong but a matter of right and always right. But the concepts entertained here only apply to the mechanics of the experiment. Speculation is only allowed to prove or disprove the theory no matter what it is. Along with the experimentation that provides proven results not sometimes or even most of the time but all the time.

"Evolution, your evolutionary clock has run out!" The science of the Bible has provided man with the reason to believe. If for no other reason, the Bible has given us a reason to seek the truth. Should I point out science is the truth and it should be? Before we could split the atom, it was necessary for man to split the skulls of the predators that sought us as a source of protein. We eventually sought the courage to believe in a higher self, a more noble purpose. The truth! Once man found the truth, he found GOD.

The moral of the story of the Bible is a simple one. We can be better than we are but only if we ascribe to the notion although we are not perfect, perfection does exist! Go and find it! For many, the "go and find it" part leads them on a deep personal relationship with their GOD. Man is a creature of faith; it is as much a part of us as the DNA that makes us different from the chimp.

For the evolutionists, their religion is a quagmire of nonbelief. All the relics, "fossils" are just as important to them, as the Mona Lisa is to fans of Leonardo da Vinci or the Pope to Catholics. It is apparently difficult for evolutionists to realize intellectual, emotional, and biological functions, which are determined by our genetics. The belief in GOD is ingrained in us also. Evolution is an argument against the truth with a fairy tale. To the atheist mind, there is no GOD because GOD doesn't talk to them so they totally discount the notion that GOD could be talking to someone else. Let us refer to it as Neanderthal narcissism.

The funny part is, while people of faith receive slings and arrows for their beliefs, atheists provide rock as hard evidence for their faith, but they are still just "essentially rocks." This belief boiled down to its essence, a worship of dead things. These rocks cannot and will not give the answers they so desperately seek. For rocks do not speak! But stark images of heathens screaming wildly dancing around a bonfire enter our minds. After all, looking to rocks for answers reminds us some kind of elaborate palm reading contest not very scientific at worst and channeling dead things at its best, which is frankly very disconcerting and very disturbing!

They attack everyone who disagrees with their religion. They feel vindicated because after all, they are more intelligent than the yokels whom they have no patience for. They spout out speculation as fact and fact as speculation. The whole time not realizing their emperor has no clothes! To the natural man, it becomes necessary to look at the basic argument what is science anyway? What are theories and what are laws? In reality, what are guiding principles we can disagree on and still be gentleman about the whole thing?

Evolutionary theory, these words are used to make a case for them, but what is a theory?

A. a hypothesis assumed for the sake of argument or investigation
B. an unproved assumption: conjecture
C. a body of theorems presenting a concise systematic view of a subject (theory of equations)

(Source: *Merriam-Webster*)

Ah, now we are getting somewhere; the secret is out and what is that secret you may ask? Evolutionary theory sounds so official, so scientific, but if you said evolutionary conjecture, you couldn't or wouldn't get nearly as much attention. Besides, spending too much time delivering their anything but GOD message, they fail to tell you that evolutionary conjecture has failed the test to be a law.

This is a simple case really; when some people, for whatever reason, hate GOD, they create a god for themselves. After all, it is trapped in our DNA. The atheist is really no different than the people they condemn, for if he were, he would need to admit we also are afraid of the dark. This simple fact leaves us with a brilliant enlightening truth. There is no light in darkness, and darkness provides no light! Therefore, my friend, it is wise to fear the dark and know there is a place of eternal light where darkness can never be found. All wise men fear the darkness, for we were born into a world of light from a place of light by the Creator of all, even the light itself! They have in fact created a story all their own. There is no GOD because man has created himself. In artwork, old bones, and the fantasy that will someday prove their story right. But will it?

Evolution and the atheist's viewpoint starkly and blindly state there is no soul, for if there were, it would be eternal! There is no afterlife, for if there were, it would be happiness everlasting. There is no joy, for if there were, that joy would feed the soul, and you could bask in the light of eternity forever. For them, the darkness provides as much information as they need to disregard the truth there is a GOD!

People of faith are portrayed by them as stupid country bumpkins, yelling hallelujahs while waving their bible in the air. Evolutionists think themselves better while they worship essentially just rocks and chimp fossils and most disturbing dead things. For us yokels, the imagery is a stark reminder of heathens dancing around stone idols. Fossils are ghost images of something that once was but is not there any longer. Your god has died and turned into a rock, and you hate the Bible believers for it.

Light is created from fire, and the simple truth is for some men and our beautiful counterparts that fire burns in our souls. Moses has seen that fire, and it is a fire that does not consume. This is a fire that feeds itself constantly and forever, for its energy source is the truth, and the truth has set us free. You have chained your soul to museums, fabricated artwork, and embraced ignorance to the truth "there is a GOD," and he forbids the worship of dead things, and it is time to get over it.

Frustration because of scanty verifiable evidence, you turn your anger on others. Artwork in a dank cave or on a canvas in the local museum, what is really the difference? If any atheist is angry at this point, let's get really simple here. Faith equals belief, simple yes! If you don't believe in GOD, then you have faith there is no GOD. Your very DNA has given you the faith that for you, rocks hold all the answers. Is it possible that some people just do not possess receptor sites for a faith in GOD? Is it missing from their DNA? Did Neanderthal have a soul? If you readily admit you have no soul, we regret to inform you you're missing something big!

We fear to believe those who would pose the question why don't you follow me? After all, I am the only one qualified to lead you, for you see, I have no soul. Isn't that your real message? We are just beast created by a mathematical impossibility into a world devoid of beauty, elation over the birth of a child, kindness at the hands of strangers, and for you, the most unlikely truth of all, there is a GOD! Sorry, my misled pagan friends, some of us know the truth simply because we have a soul, and that soul hears GOD calling us to eternity as a mother would call her children to dinner.

Faith is based on one's own deep personal belief. Where do you derive your faith from? Rocks, museums, your literature, *Origin of the Species*? Therein lies the truth, your narcissism. It has led you to believe through smoke, mirrors, and artwork, your ancestors created themselves. Man created himself! We get it, halleluiah power to the rock? If some of us don't get misty-eyed, forgive us. We know some self-righteously blind themselves to the truth. It is much easier to find what you are looking for than it is to find something you weren't looking for. The real truth is, you can't find GOD in a hole! This is especially difficult when you don't know what it is you are looking for in the first place. A lifetime spent hiding from GOD will never help you find him; you are a curse on to yourselves.

How come Newton has a law and Einstein only has a theory? Was Newton smarter than Einstein? No, the mechanics of proving a theory will eventually lead to the truthfulness of the theory, and it will graduate to a law. Newton's law is provable through experimentation and has been carried out enough times to be justified as a law. If you slam on your brakes in your car too hard, you will prove it to yourself.

For Einstein's theory of relativity to be a law, you could prove that in your car also, but only if your car could travel at the speed of light. But don't forget your wristwatch or you will miss a conclusive result, your watch will stop. The Einstein theory works because it is observable and appears to be the truth. Not until it is proven conclusively with testable data, verifiable reproducible data, will it ever be a law. The same is true for evolution, but unlike Einstein's theory, attempts to test evolution are unlikely.

> So science has tossed the use of "law" in favor of "theory." This "theory" does not mean "hypothesis," which is a speculation. In this case, think of music theory—definitely not a hypothesis, but a working set of rules that define a body of knowledge. Read more at Suite101: Theory vs. Hypothesis vs. Law: Unraveling the Confusion of Important Terminology.
> (Source: http://physics.suite101.com/article. cfm/theory vs hypothesis vs law#ixzz0tT5b0Hf5)

For the atheist, it is a difficult concept to understand. They do not have a lack of faith in core religious dogma, but a rigid faith in something else, the Darwinism dogma. In essence, your belief is simply placed in something else. The evolutionist has placed their faith in an argument, assumed for the sake of argumentation or experimentation. How could we say it differently? "You are basing your belief on an unproven assumption." You might have proven it to yourself in your mind, possibly many times. Your conclusion is inconclusive because it isn't measured against the scientific method. Dare we say the truth, evolution is anything but scientific!

Basically, you are providing an argument as fact, for the sake of argumentation, to prove the unproven assumption, of your atheist viewpoint. Children and adults do this all the time; it is commonly known as a lie. After all, if you are an atheist, you are really pagans; you worship perceived nonexistent ancestors. All the fossil relics of rocks, stones, and your evolutionary brothers the chimp are a delusion created to fill the gap in your souls. I wish I could help you because all the rocks in the world will not fill that gap. All of this on a blind faith more absurd than the Christians, Jews, and others you condemn. The sciences you value as truth are rapidly proving you wrong.

We can only have evidence of what we see in our atheist friends. If you hold the viewpoint of everyone around you that doesn't share your position is stupid, or as in the words of some grand high priest of the atheist cult. We cannot help but wonder about your motives, friends (Wicked).

Mr. Dawkins easily throws around the label of belief in a higher power as a mental condition. Mr. Dawkins, you are totally ignoring the facts surrounding the case as it relates to us real Homo sapiens. In light of the fact of growing nonevidence and in particular the lack of transitional fossils. Evolution is running out of time as science will end the experiment and probably sooner than you might think. Ignoring has its roots in ignorance, which is the result of evolutionary belief because you are ignoring the results of the evolutionary experiment and its results, which to date are none.

In the words of Mr. Charles Darwin, he himself has in his own words condemned this fraudulent theory. He made a judgment on the subject before it could be proven or disproven. What did Mr. Darwin have to say about the subject on the question of transitional fossils? Let us explore and answer this question with the simplest formula—Mr. Darwin's own words.

"The case at present (Evolution) must remain inexplicable and may be truly argued as a valid argument against the views here entertained" (Source: Charles Darwin).

Darwin himself has ended the experiment based on the lack of evidence. It is truly sad, but to continue to waste time on a lost cause is just silly. To the evolutionists, they are always just one fossil find from the real honest to goodness evolutionary truth. Despite the slings and arrows that will undoubtedly find me from the evolutionist, I will place my viewpoint in opposition to evolutionary theory. Charles Darwin himself has spoken to the fact that I do have a valid argument for that argument was laid out by the genius of Charles Darwin!

It may be our evolutionary friends may condemn Charles Darwin to hell as their grand high priest. I see a different picture of Charles as a man who provided an experiment an alternate viewpoint as to the workings of the universe as he understood it. He outlined the experiment its predictions and outcomes and, as a matter of fact, has proven there is a GOD. The joke is over and the only one laughing is Charles Darwin himself; the rest of you have fooled yourselves with fake science. The experiment is over. Charles has provided an experiment that has played out and the conclusion…there is a GOD. Get over it.

My position and the position of many others offer this fact; we are not in opposition to evolution for at its basic core, it is simply an idea and it always has been just an idea. The truth is, these ideas are only good until a new idea corrects the problems with the old idea. As far as I know, evolution cannot prove or disprove if Australopithecus had a penis bone! They have not provided a chimp foot with signs of the big toe shifting position or shoulder sockets gradually moving down or any anomaly that truly separates us from the great apes under transition.

The only argument that can be made here is the honest and rightful viewpoint that the scientist who creates the experiment has a right to define the parameters to the experiment. This should include what would terminate the experiment because of a lack of evidence. Mr. Darwin did that, he laid out his hypothesis…man came from apes? He then provided a formula…apes slowly evolved to humans? Evidence for the truth of this hypothesis would be fossils showing slow evolutionary change. It is not found in the fossil record nor will it ever be for it is nonexistent and a lie.

Every presidential candidate professes their belief in GOD. Most candidates do and the reason is a simple one. This proclamation states to the voting public, I am not an atheist and I do have a soul, and I make myself accountable to GOD. Why would this be important to the voting public? Well, if you look at our history, the most prolific, sick psychopaths in the history of man were atheists. Men like Joseph Stalin, Adolph Hitler, and the real chairman of the board MAO. When you say you are an atheist immediately, visions of death camps, unrestrained murder, and death fill our minds and mostly because it is true. With the lack of any moral foundation, it is easy to entertain if there are no consequences, no afterlife, no judgment, and most importantly, no GOD.

Mr. Dawkins has proclaimed judgment on all the nonbelievers of your stone-worshipping cult. If believers in GOD are truly wicked, due to the fact we don't follow the lie, then exactly how wicked, Mr. Dawkins? Like put in a mental hospital wicked, or more like put in prison wicked, or like Stalin wicked taken to a shower stall where your brains are blown out wicked, or MAO wicked where you are simply left to starve to death wicked. If anyone wants to claim Hitler was a Christian and his killing spree based on Christian beliefs, then consider this, no one and I mean no one believes that except you!

If we do not buy into your rock-worshipping cult, it is because we have seen the results of its practitioners. Human death and suffering on a massive scale. The worship of dead things leads to the inevitable conclusion—more dead things. Could it be atheists merely think of us as chimps in a human suit, something really not that important? If you don't believe in GOD, your view on human life is not unlike blowing your nose or wiping the sweat from your brow just a minor distraction. Remember this, all of this while proclaiming I have no soul.

Killing innocents is just a part of natural selection with them doing the selecting. In reality, it is just cruel despots providing onlookers with a view into their sick psychopathic minds. If you don't believe in GOD, then you don't believe in sin; if you don't believe in sin, murder, death, and genocide, just don't seem that bad. Let's put it this way, you are embracing a faith that brings death and destruction, and in your imaginings we can't buy in.

Man's confession to not be perfect puts him on the road to perfection. What is perfection? Science is the closest we can come up with inside the construct of the human mind, or the concept of a higher being GOD! Therein lies the truth of it, the road to perfection can only be found in the examples of the concept of perfection. For us, GOD is perfect!

Before science, we had GOD, the humanistic idea of perfection and arguably the road to truth. You might think how this could relate to our present condition in relation to the world we live in. Well, here it is. It gives us hope in the GOD that has provided for us the beauty of this world. The greatest examples of the perfection of GOD are in the perfect beauty in which He created all things.

This world is abounding with the perfection some no longer desperately seek. These people have found perfection in GOD. Where is the hope in evolution? Denial of the majesty of GOD and the beauty with which He created the world cannot be replaced with just old bones artwork and fake supposition. Obviously, evolution and its teachings lead us on a path that waste time, money, and energy while trying to prove man has created himself. Evolution can come up with new and improved speculation, with more wishful thinking than should be allowed, but at what cost?

If you are basing your nonbelief in GOD on evolutionary theory, then know this, you are basing your beliefs on an argument for the purposes of experimentation. This has not played out favorably for evolution. "No proof." Sad but true. In an imperfect world, we were confronted with the obstacles of imperfection on a daily basis. Our belief demanded that we seek perfection, whatever that is and ultimately the truth and most certainly GOD.

It is in our DNA because the GOD of creation put it there. We seek order and purpose, and a GOD who knows and understands these concepts as well. For some of the lucky ones, the search is over; we have found perfection, his name is GOD. It is our desire to know the truth, understand the truth and ultimately the GOD who created everything. This is for the simplest of reasons because we were made in his image and likeness.

Cruel indulgence into one's own special intelligence provides the practitioner with a path to his or her own megalomania. It is sad but true, the evolutionist has denied the importance of speculation and sought to provide it as fact. This is because speculation is only valid when it leads to proof, hence the scientific method. Mr. Dawkins explains his viewpoint on evolution and takes the time to let us know how he feels about it.

"It is absolutely safe to say that if you meet someone who claims not to believe in evolution, that person is ignorant, stupid, or insane (or wicked)" (Source: Richard Dawkins. "Put your Money on Evolution." New York Times. April 9, 1999, p. 35).

Simply because chimps like humans have fingerprints? If Mr. Dawkins has made a statement, it is a statement of intolerance and judgment. Poor hurt, little man! He has labeled the most important part of the experiment ignorant, stupid, and insane (or wicked) the alternate viewpoint, how sad he mocks the science he worships. He claims intelligence but throws out the most important part of the experiment the argument against his hypothetical theory. The hopeless, helpless self-indulgent and a puritanical belief in the temples of rocks, leave us believers cold and unfulfilled. At its root, Mr. Dawkins, should I ever need advice, I will seek it from a more reliable source and one who does not worship at the altar of dead things. All this while claiming he has no soul, and the truth is you may be right.

To find right or wrong is perfection itself; to deny the experiment leads to ignorance intolerance and the death of the reason. To be unique and most importantly the quest for truth is an important part in the quest for perfection. Skepticism is the most vital part of the scientific method. Without it, we are no better than the animals we look down upon. Skepticism leads to reason and reason to the truth. To deny the truth is far worse than believing something that isn't true. We get it, but if it's good for science to object to an alternate viewpoint, then this removes the most important part of the experiment. This is at its essence the holy grail of science, which is to be skeptical. But have no fear, Mr. Dawkins will tell us what to believe and at the cost of being wicked for believing otherwise.

The reason to believe the truth, the real truth, is not something wrapped up and shoved in a can for semi popular consumption of the pagan few. But the high road that tells the truth and its practitioners can know the truth of it also. The evolutionary experiment is dead for its conclusions have killed it as outlined by its inventor Charles Darwin.

The value of science is best understood with the notion that if we can ascribe a discipline of perfection to our sciences, we can find the truth. Science is as solid as a rock as long as we ascribe to the notion, "We understood the rock of ages before we discovered the age of rocks." Thank you, William Jennings Bryant, this quote is truer than nonexistent transitional fossils some folks are still looking for.

The value of GOD is best understood with this notion. That if we can apply a discipline of perfection to ourselves, we can find out not only who we are, but also where we are going, and GOD willing the most importantly part of the puzzle for our lives, "how to get there." "The perfection ascribed to science is no less perfect than the values we place on our belief in the GOD of perfection." It is GOD who demands of us perfection itself. GOD has provided us a vehicle to get there with His Holy Bible.

The Bible and the notion that the same science used by GOD can be duplicated by his creation man are exhilarating. I am not anymore afraid of science being wrong than I am of the concept of the GOD who created everything being wrong. Science is catching up to GOD by proving Him right. Wright and wrong are constructs of our own human experience. Perfection is something to aspire to, and so we have a GOD of perfection, himself like science, the holy grail of truth.

"Be ye therefore perfect, even as you're Father which is in heaven is perfect" (Source: The Holy Bible, Matthew 5:48).

Chapter 7

○

The God with Fifty Names

In the pages of human history, it is evident that man has always found it necessary to worship the unknown forces of the surrounding miracles that confronted him on his dramatic walk through life. Most people understand present-day religious practices and dismiss them as commonplace. If we look at the history behind the opposition, this is what you will find.

Marduk or Baal is an ancient god also known as Bel represented by the dragon with the forked tongue. He is most notably known as the god with fifty names. Marduk's star was Jupiter, and his sacred animals were horses, dogs, and especially the so-called dragon with the forked tongue. The dragon is a recurring theme in many religions, but to be sure, we are usually talking about a dark subject anytime the word dragon enters into the conversation.

It is interesting to note that criminals use aliases because they are constantly looking to change their identity. Any god that changes his name fifty times has something to hide. "Yes, the dragon." We will get to this role later, but for now, let's understand this hellish pagan cult. No matter what name you call him by, he obviously requires death from his worshippers. Apparently, death, pain, and torture are the things this guy specializes in. His disdain for his human worshippers is recorded in the symbolism and the requirements Bel put upon his followers.

The Greek historian Herodotus tells us that this God is known by other names Jupiter for the Romans, Zeus for the Greeks, and Mazda for the Persians, and Ammon for the Egyptians. Yes, this guy gets around and as you will see, he changes names but his MO (modus operandi) is always the same. Once Satan gets his man in charge, then the killing starts. Pagan human sacrifice or just the act of war make this god an easily understood entity, and no matter what name he goes by, his methods are clearly demonstrated in the death toll he requires.

Also included in this document are the fifty names of Marduk. In Enûma Elish, a civil war between the gods was growing to a climactic battle…Marduk was depicted as a human, often with his symbol the snake-dragon which he had taken over from the god Tishpak (Source: Marduk—Wikipedia https://en.wikipedia.org/wiki/Marduk)

It is interesting to note that the powers of this god were described in the following terms. He was referred to as the sky god; he had the ability to shut up the heavens so it would not rain, and he could cause earthquakes! Many other calamities were attributed to him, but most noteworthy was he demanded human sacrifice and especially children. Clearly, the GOD of Abraham Isaac and Jacob have made judgments against such practices and for obvious reasons.

Baal/Amon priests would run around wildly and cut themselves with knives in rites of self-inflicted injury. The masses of people would offer up their children to appease Bel Marduk (Lord Marduk). If you miss the connection, this guy sounds strangely like Lucifer who hates us and is happy at the death or destruction of anyone of us. It is his plan to supersede the plan of GOD with a plan of his own. As we will see, this plan is to destroy GOD's creation.

Let us pay special attention to the self-inflicted injury, but you will see it again later in our story. You will soon learn the correlation and oddly enough how it affects us today. Baal was also a perverted god; sexual relations were a big part of his following. They even ran prostitution rings in their temples. If these practices sound occult, it is because they were and still are. The more debase and perverted, the better as it insured followers were a big part of their own sin and eventual punishment. The priestesses would give sexual favors for cash, and the resulting perversion would supply new children for the fires of Baal.

Compounded by the fact that the murder of children is appalling, the child who is innocent gets a ticket straight to heaven. The worshippers are not so lucky; at worst, they have passed judgment and damnation for eternity on themselves at best idolatry and eternal condemnation. So appeasing Baal required a human sacrifice, the firstborn of the one making the sacrifice would usually do. The priests of Baal appealed to their god in rites of wild abandon, these included loud, ecstatic cries and as stated earlier, self-inflicted injury. Given the medical practices of the time and the general unsanitary conditions, I am sure many followers succumbed to their religious practices from horrendous infections. This offered a special twist to worshipping a god who hated his followers and nonfollowers alike.

Well, what's the draw to such a hellish cult?

1.   Perversion
2.   Murder

If it sounds like it isn't much fun, then I would say you are a religious person with moral bearing and fortitude. Yea, a real party pooper, but let's not forget, there is a certain segment of ancient society that would buy in. These gods and their prodigy led lives full of deceit, adultery, and at times, homosexual activity was not off the menu. They were not the meek and regal gods depicted on the walls of Egypt. Stories about them involve a struggle for dominance, usually over any people who would worship them.

If we look closely enough at the end result of their ten-year war, death and plague were a commonplace occurrence for their worshippers. Entire civilizations disappeared under their rule. Baal worshippers soon found self-inflicted damage; this resulted in the worship of a god that just wanted all humans dead in the first place. In their stories, these gods played tricks and cheated one another. Out and out, deceit and lies were common tools used by the Ammon/Baal cult gods, and illustrations of their followers committing human atrocities were commonplace.

These gods found particular enjoyment in deceiving their followers into killing other humans. These leaders, like the pharaohs, were kept around until their usefulness was over. Like a discarded pawn, at which time, the pharaoh was either deceived into a war they lost or just died of natural causes. The living gods of Egypt viewed the common man as just cannon fodder for the fires of Ammon/Baal. Oftentimes, the same god with different names would have his followers killing each other on opposite sides of a conflict. If you are losing the description and the eventual outcome, this god has demonstrated his hatred for mankind over and over often in the history of mankind. Death and killing is the true nature of these demons; the object of their obsession was the death of us, the human race.

If, as stated earlier, ancient people contained greater concentrations of Neanderthal DNA in their genetic makeup, then the general population would be, could we say less civilized? The possibility is that the sociopath was commonplace and in larger concentrations in the general population. What is a sociopath? If you are not sure what it means, then I would never suggest you use it as a defense in a felony trial. The judge will send you to prison with the rest of the criminals. Prisons serve as warehousing for societies, sociopaths.

There is a certain segment of societies that are not too concerned with the rest of the population and would rather turn to crime than lead peaceful productive lives. Their logic is short-circuited into simply what is best for them. Can we just call it what it appears to be "Neanderthal tendencies?" These problems are compounded when you put the criminals in charge, which was obviously the case in the worship of Baal. It may be pure speculation on my part, but given the attitude of the people of those days, if strength equaled power, then the guy with the most Neanderthal in his genetic makeup would usually win. It was a top-down society and being at bottom could be fatal. The only flaw in this plan was the genetic make-up of Homo sapiens made us proliferate in greater numbers. Nevertheless, Neanderthal never went extinct; his genetic structure still exists in some of us today.

Let us consider this, with murderers, prostitutes, perverts, and thieves in charge, things were pretty bad. Are we getting the picture? It is literally society turned upside down. Criminals in charge of the country with no desirable act in their minds left undone. With the use of murder, intimidation, blackmail, and torture, these wicked gods flourished in the ancient world. Get along with the cult or they may require your firstborn as a sacrifice, this would help prove your loyalty to the cult. It should be noted that given the Neanderthals propensity for lawlessness, cruel and deceptive gods were something he could identify with.

Oh boy, where do we sign up? Sounds like the worshippers of Baal were having a pretty good time. The reason here is, it was practiced everywhere. But not so fast! There was opposition to this predominant cult in the ancient Middle Eastern world. This GOD was much different as we will see. Soon, we will know that the practices of this GOD set him in a category extremely different from the other cults of the day.

It has been said that the Egyptians just didn't find the true GOD that exciting because he did not have the baggage that the Ammon/Baal gods did. After all, gods dismembering each other and killing for sport just was more exciting to the sociopath of that day. Neanderthal tendencies or a god, even a criminal god, they could really believe in.

Now, let's take a look at the largest and longest run cult in the Middle Eastern world. Egypt? Yes, the home of the pharaohs. You know, those men who thought they were living gods? The message is eerily not unlike the message of evolution in a land where Amon/Baal ruled, and a man could be a living god. In the evolutionary narrative, this is how the miracle of miracles happened and through the deception of evolution, man has created himself. Sure he has!

But who did they worship? Ammon Ra was the god they considered a rough and tumble kind of guy. Let's remember Ammon was, is, and has always been Baal. Ammon/Baal was and, as you will see, still is a pretty good way for people to do whatever they want. The incestuous relationships were entertained through the royal cult and most likely practiced by the common folk as well. Consider the Leviticus law, interbreeding not only causes deformations, but it would also strengthen the Neanderthal bloodline, reproducing greater and greater concentrations of Neanderthal progeny.

Most people would shudder at the prospect of going to church to look for a prostitute. But making a god to this practice was simply ritualized sinning. Every manner of lust was provided for by the priestesses for a price. But how could we draw a correlation to the pagan practices of then and the aftermath of the Neanderthal footprint of the past? Evolutionists marvel at the heads of Neanderthal and ignore the skulls of the pharaohs. Yes, very oddly shaped, reminiscent of Neanderthal only oftentimes stranger. It should be remembered inbreeding causes skull deformations and quite possibly in an attempt to copy and strengthen the Neanderthal bloodline.

Moses's objection to incest had a specific goal—this being Neanderthal genetics were allowed to flourish by a sexual relationship with family members increased the likelihood of Neanderthal genetics to duplicate and increase in number providing a creature that very well could have been more Neanderthal and less human. Skull deformity in the offspring of children derived from incest are common, as well as albinism. Yes, those children are more commonly born white than the rest of the population who doesn't practice incest.

Albinism is found in the general population. However, its incidence in the children of incest are more likely due to the fact the gene providing for melanin often finds a blank where a melanin in normal relationships finds the gene of color. Moses was given the commandant to prevent Neanderthal making a comeback and clearly, thoughts of Neanderthal being human were discounted by their extreme practices—human sacrifice, cannibalism, murder and, war; common traits of the true Neanderthal.

Fast forward to way back then, and oddly enough, there was another GOD in Egypt. He was named El, and the Egyptians considered El a secondary God and not that powerful. But El is listed as a God nonetheless. During the times of the pharaohs, El had a following among the Hebrew slaves in Egypt. The original Hebrews came through the lineage of Abraham, and he came from the area of

Sumer with traditions and a belief much different than the worshippers of Ammon/Baal.

How did El get in there, I mean how did he get airtime in light of the master of the sky god Baal/Ammon? Killing and murdering his way to the top of the heap. The fork-tongued dragon was the prominent deity and held that top spot for centuries. I mean really how could a GOD that did not require the sacrifice of humans be that powerful? How could a kind and gentle GOD work His way to the top? Remember, Ammon/Baal, the bully god of the bullies, was completely opposite of El. El rose to prominence simply because of one of his followers proved his power. Have you ever heard of him? This man's name was Moses and was raised in the house of pharaoh.

The Bible doesn't mix words, and its pages are seething with the enemy of GOD, the dragon or the serpent with the forked tongue. The picture is clear, and the worship of the dragon was forbidden by the followers of El. History time and the Bible brings us to Joseph? Yes, that's the guy who rose from a young boy, sold by his brothers into slavery, to a position second only to the pharaohs. Four hundred years before Moses, Joseph brought El with him as the Bible/Torah tells us. GOD saved him with divine intervention several times, but his wisdom and judgment brought him from slavery to the court of Egypt.

Joseph protected Egypt from famine with the information El provided him. I suppose if any God protected you for seven years of starvation, you might consider him a deity. The Egyptians allowed the name but didn't think much of the Hebrew GOD. After all, he was the God of slaves. If it kept the slaves happy and making bricks, what could the harm be? He wasn't a very entertaining GOD because he forbids the practice of murder, rape, thievery, and deception. For the Ammon/Baal die-hard fan's opposition to incest was the last straw for them.

El was the direct opposite of the ruling contender Ammon Ra. El was merciful and kind, and the Hebrew slaves prayed for his help to remove them from the mud pits of Egypt. Ammon Ra, the god that was ruling Egypt at this time, was predominantly a sociopathic and psychopathic god. Ra had an appeal for Egypt's mass population, but the Pharaoh was considered by the people to be a god also. Considering their skulls, it is easy to see why they appeared not to be people commonly produced by the general population. It is easy to see why they wore that elaborate head wear common for Egyptian royalty. He, Ammon Ra, kept the people in line with the threat of death looming large.

Moses shows up one day demanding, "Pharaoh, let my people go." Pharaoh knew who El was because he knew who Moses was, his adopted brother who refused to believe in Amon. In fact, Moses chose to leave Egypt rather than indulge in rights and rituals of the fork-tongued dragon. For Moses saw the result of murder and slavery on his people. In light of the suffering of the Hebrew people, El heard their suffering and molded Moses into the intermediary between God and the Hebrew people who eventually set GOD's people free. I am sure at this point, evolutionists may wonder where I am going with this. It is clear that history is something they are interested in, but necessity makes them look much further back. Could this be because it is easier to cloud the issue without a written history, without oration, and without the true history of mankind? But just as El was too dull for the ruling upper class of Egypt, he is also too dull for the rock worshippers.

The Hebrews claim is that the name Moses comes from the root word to draw from the water, but the Egyptians had a very similar name (Thutmose), which means the son of Thoth or Thoth is born. Thoth is the Egyptian god of writing, magic, wisdom, and the moon. The Hebrews to this day use the cycles of the moon to maintain their calendar. Thutmose II is the only pharaoh's mummy to display cysts, possible evidence of plagues which spread through the Egyptian Empire at the time of the great plagues.

If you wonder how the pharaoh could harden his heart at the unfolding of the ten plagues, then let's consider their first meeting. Moses demand for his people's freedom, and the pharaoh must have laughed himself silly. El, come on really? For the pharaoh, it was a clash of the gods; for Moses, it was inevitable. That old book of fairy tales tells us that Moses, the son of a Hebrew slave, was adopted by the daughter of the pharaoh. Was there ever a Moses or is this a fairy tale? It is interesting to note Thutmose is not a Hebrew name but an Egyptian name while Moses means to draw from the water. Bithiah, Moses's adoptive mother, is known in the Bible with a Hebrew name meaning daughter of Yah or daughter of GOD.

It should be remembered that the pharaohs were considered living gods, and giving in to the unseen GOD would make the pharaoh appear to be a real loser. In particular and most pointedly, especially any lower god of a bunch of lowlife slaves! How could he explain to all his concubines and prostitutes his fear of a GOD more powerful than himself? Perhaps he feared the priest of the cult would murder him, but the record is pretty clear. He would not give in.

The GOD of Hebrew slaves, the GOD who let them be put into slavery in the first place, how could he save them? Perhaps it never occurred to Pharaoh that El was chastising his belligerent children and inevitably, the empire of Egypt would be laid low at the intervention of El. Like the beautiful scent of the rose, it smells best when it is crushed. Apparently, GOD knows us better than we know ourselves. When left alone to our own devices, we will get ourselves in trouble.

Apparently, it never occurred to Pharaoh that the GOD of Jacob could be very powerful, but he in fact was the GOD who brought mighty Egypt to her punishment and condemnation. This isn't as thin and frail as evolutionary theory but is a historical fact. The god Pharaoh didn't laugh for long when El brought Egypt to its knees, destroyed his army, and left Egypt starving and easy pickings for the other murdering psycho, rapist, and idolaters in the surrounding kingdoms.

It should also be remembered that the Hebrew people had traditional and written laws that required them to wash themselves before religious practice could take place. It should be easy to figure out in a land where plagues and death was running ramped, the act of being clean could have saved thousands. When those laws were not known or overlooked by the Egyptians, death from disease was a certainty. Hygiene is considered the science of health and despite evolutionary thought or reason, yes, it was invented by a man who lived over three thousand years ago by a man named Moses.

Ignorance, it appears, has its price! Make no mistake, ignorance has its roots; in the simple word, to ignore not like stupid or dumb ignorance is to ignore the truth, and it appears the Bible is the true history of man. Consider this, it provides a blueprint to not just spiritual matters but guidelines for even hygiene. During a time when Egyptian historians complained about the stench from dead animals lying in the street to what women were doing with alligator feces to prevent pregnancy. Their Hebrew counterparts had strict religious practices of keeping filth away from the Hebrew people.

(Source: http://www.cbsnews.com/pictures/15-most-bizarre-medical-treatment-ever/5/)

In ancient Egypt, *the contraceptive of choice was crocodile* dung. *Dried* dung *was inserted into the* vagina.

Moses gave with specific guidelines on how to properly and safely dispose of important health problems and prevent many public biohazards. The picture should be becoming clear on why the Hebrew people did not succumb to the plagues of Egypt. With this thought firmly in place, they had a science to protect them before science was ever conceived. His name was GOD, and every aspect of human health was not only a matter of written faith but also a matter of fact.

Why we don't marvel at the fact that the GOD who promised to protect us gave us morality laws, hygiene laws, dietary laws is totally astounding to me. All this from a man who said he talked to GOD for forty days on a mountaintop! Do you think he didn't? I will put my faith in this story gladly before evolution comes up with its first experiment to prove itself. Are you feeling a little cheated here? You should be. How you can know the truth when it is constantly being covered in lies? I suppose the most convinced of us might look at this problem and say we have been deceived. Is there a deceiver in our midst?

Again, the laws of GOD provided for disease with the following guidelines. Leviticus 7:19–21 provide not only for the uncleanness of dead things, but also on animals considered unfit to eat. The list goes on and on, but each law provides not only spiritual and ethical rules to maintain a healthy society, but also important measures to continue safety on the matters of disease.

If I am going too fast, I apologize, but you can get the same story in the New King James Version of the Bible or the Torah. It is a lot longer than my story, but if you think I am missing something, please do tell. The point to be made here is that this GOD of Hebrew slaves (Yahweh) or El ran his rules in that day in complete opposition to the murdering, prostitute cults surrounding the twelve tribes of Israel. When I say outnumbered, folks, I am not kidding. But you cannot argue with results, and GOD provided those results with his specialized laws.

This GOD El had rules—a lot of rules—over six hundred if you count them all, so let's get started. First, rule number one. Just kidding, let's talk about the most interesting ones. The Leviticus 18 law provided for the genetic rules and regulations from back breeding into the distant gene pool and dredging up the Neanderthal equivalent of a very dangerous species long past. While following this law not only provided for the protection of the human race as a whole, but it also provided for the prevention of the return of the Nephilim/Neanderthal. These creatures are also known by the following names Neanderthal, giants, Goliath of Gath, and men of old, men of renown.

> Then the Lord spoke to Moses, saying, "Speak to the children of Israel, and say to them: 'I am the Lord your God. According to the doings of the land of Egypt, where you dwelt, you shall not do; and according to the doings of the land of Canaan, where I am bringing you, you shall not do; nor shall you walk in their ordinances. You shall observe my judgments and keep my ordinances, to walk in them: I am the Lord your God. You shall therefore keep my statutes and my judgments, which if a man does, he shall live by them: I am the Lord." (Lev. 18:1–5)

Apparently, GOD provided for separation from people considered to be troublesome for his chosen people. Was there more here than meets the eye? Could it possibly be that GOD knew the problems with other members of the human race corrupted with the demon seed? It is obvious that GOD provided for the insulation of his people against the other corrupted people of the day.

Baal was the Canaanite god and nearly identical to Ammon in every respect. The origins, while cloudy, represent a psychotic deity with a propensity for human flesh and human suffering. I am trusting Herodotus on this one. Remember the god with fifty names! The Hebrew people were surrounded by the believers of Ammon/Baal and refused to worship this psychotic mass murderer. Can you blame them? The Egyptian gods kept them slaves for four hundred years!

You can look it up if you want to, but it makes pretty clear sense that what went on in Vegas doesn't really stay in Vegas, at least not with El (Yahweh). You have free will but are held accountable for how you use it. The Leviticus 18 rule is the one that forbids sexual relations with close family members. Because both Christians and Jews believe in the Old Testament, we take that rule to heart.

It is a hallmark of the GOD El that we do not condone or revel in the flesh of family members. It's bad business. Let's consider sexual relations between cousins; it is the equal to sexual relations between half siblings. The Leviticus rule, when violated, was considered detestable, and the people of GOD were strictly forbidden from indulging in it or worshipping gods that allow it. In fact, even consorting with the believers of it is not allowed in any way, shape, or form.

Sounds like the religion of murders, prostitutes, and psychopaths was not something El wanted you to be involved with. Pretty good advice and the local cops will pick you up if you hang around with folks like this. It is known as guilt by association today. What is known is that Yahweh was completely different from the other surrounding deities. In contrast to the blood thirsty child killers, the concept of a loving GOD was in opposition to the ruling aristocracy.

The GOD Yahweh not only forbid the killing of children, it was considered an abdominal act of such a debase nature; it was literally unforgivable. Further investigation reveals the GOD Yahweh is a loving although strict GOD with special laws and attributes that separated him from his contemporaries.

The GOD of the Bible, time and time again, came out on top; those who turned their hearts to strange gods were punished oftentimes through their own idolatry. When GOD's laws were not followed, the result would find the people unclean. Oftentimes, the mass population would suffer from the filthy habits of the pagan gods. GOD's judgment would eventually find them. It is interesting to note while pagan religious writings almost always depict their gods as helping the heroes of the day, Yahweh instead helped the common man and blessed those common people who worshipped him. Yahweh's oppressed people sought his justice, and many apparently found it. While his counterpart Ammon/Baal just wanted war, blood, and death.

It is his purpose that we need to find in our life. Should we fall or fail, we should get up, dust ourselves off, and learn from our mistakes. Keep moving in a righteous direction and help others to find their purpose also. It is fair to say that Yahweh/El is the complete opposite of the pagan god Ammon Ra in every detail. Yahweh speaks to the hearts of men requiring of them patience and love for their fellow man while Ammon/Baal just wants you dead, dying, starving, and in the end, in hell with him.

Murder, rape, and idolatry are forbidden, and in fact, those who do as they want are punished for their crimes against the laws and people of the true and living GOD. Where did Yahweh come from? The Old Testament and the Torah answer us emphatically on that question:

> So when the Lord saw that he turned aside to look, God called to him from the midst of the bush and said, "Moses, Moses!"
>
> And he said, "Here I am."
>
> Then He said, "Do not draw near this place. Take your sandals off your feet, for the place where you stand is holy ground."

> Moreover He said, "I am the God of your father—the God of Abraham, the God of Isaac, and the God of Jacob." And Moses hid his face, for he was afraid to look upon God. (Exod. 3:4–6, NKJV)

It is interesting to note that Moses wrote the Torah not with the stories of creation from the Egyptian creation story, but from the Sumerian accounts of GOD, which are by far much older. This leads us to question, did Moses choose a story he liked better or is there a divine intervention here? I prefer the latter. Some of the Levitical laws are millennia past where we are even today. Refusal to follow them leads us on a path that indulges in paganism.

We should remember that the Sumerian account is much older than the Egyptian account and that Moses prepared the lineages of the people who worshipped Yahweh from the beginning of the world. Since the creation of man, it is very possible the Sumerian account might in fact be a written record of what Moses knew and was told to be true. Was it because it was true? When the Romans burned the library in Alexandria, no one will ever know how much of the history of man was lost to the flames. Let us not forget Moses was an educated man and may have had access to many writings turned into ash at the hands of the conquering Romans. But just may be, Moses talked to his GOD and of the utmost importance, his GOD talked to him.

If I am getting too preachy here, it is just to illustrate that the common thinking of the man on the street of that day, it wasn't all that much different than the logic of many of the guys on death row today. Let's reflect in today's language who Ammon Ra was—"an arrogant detestable bully with a hate of anything that furthered the true destiny of man." Ammon/Baal required human sacrifice and had his followers commit acts that doomed them to hell. It really doesn't matter on a pagan altar or on the battlefield Ammon/Baal required death as a prelude to his being worshipped. What a deal death, dying, and suffering on a scale only equaled by its results.

It will be brought up that accounts of Egyptian pagan ritualized murder was something unclear in the pages of history. But if you think you have me here, Egypt's propensity for war, killing, and slavery cannot be disputed and stands unparalleled in the annals of the ancient world. When we reflect on the history of bullies, names appear like Genghis Khan, all the rulers of the ancient Middle East right through the Caesar's, the pagan rulers of Europe right down to famous guys like Hitler, Stalin, and Chairman Mao Zedong. All regions of the world where at one time not only did Neanderthal live in these areas, but he also spread his seed there also.

These men were responsible for the deaths of countless millions. The sheer numbers of death and suffering stagger the imagination. World War II, sixty million died. "Thanks, Hitler." Joseph Stalin, the beaten and abused son of a cobbler, was credited with the deaths of twenty million people after the war! While sixty million perished as the results of World War II, some estimates run higher. If you look at the progeny never born because of their deaths, the estimates are mind numbing. If the picture isn't clear, worshipping a god that demands the death of his worshippers is madness itself. Suicide, the ultimate wrong of any society today, was the main goal by the practitioners of ancient paganism.

Chairman Mao, not to be undone by his western rivals, was responsible for the deaths of another eighty million people, mostly women and children who simply were left to starved to death. In all, 140,000,000 people's lives were lost and for what? "These men's hate for the weak and innocent strangely mirror the fork-tongued dragon." Satan appears, time and time again, destroying any humanity unfortunate enough to be alive at the same time period of these despotic psychopathic killers." For the believers in evolution, they provide themselves the opportunity to believe in rocks and dead things. They would have you believe in it also, but by the actions and admittance, they have no soul; it is clear to see whose bidding they are doing.

The picture to be painted here is simply this, if Satan exists, he seems to be a harmless figment of our overactive imagination, a boogeyman story—that is, until Satan moves through the veil to attain human flesh. Then suddenly, this boogeyman, terrible and psychotic, gets to work killing us, GOD's creation. The parallel to be gleaned here is that time and time again, despotic leaders hate humanity, either in part or in total. Their reasoning needs no further investigation as they seem to propagate the same agenda as the forked tonged dragon death to mankind.

Hitler, a psychotic despot of Christian origins; Stalin, a club-footed, withered armed atheist; and the real chairman of the board Mao. This man Mao starved without regret women and children to death; he was also an atheist. Common denominators were insanity and greed. These psychopaths of different political ideas and against each other at times were not satisfied until their governance ended in the deaths of millions.

> Hitler A: The fuehrer had many secrets beginning with his lineage—who his grandfather was. The question is unanswered today. Most probably, there was an incident of incest in his family. His father married his own niece. Hitler hid this fact his whole life. He was terribly afraid the truth would be uncovered. The second secret is Hitler's relationship with both men and women—his suppressed homosexuality and fear of intimacy with the opposite sex. The result was a general discord with his being and resentment against the entire world. It seems the only person Hitler experienced feelings for (including sexual) was his own niece Geli Raubal. Raubal committed suicide in 1931.
>
> (Source: fpp.co.uk Historian Leonid Mlechin the book Sexual disorder led to Hitler's rise to power.)

We need to say more on Herr Hitler, his fear of being found out as a product of an incestuous father and his niece was lessened when he himself found that his sexual desires turned to his own niece just as his father had done. Like father like son? Only the genetics can disprove the theory for sure, but Hitler never reproduced himself. What is also likely his distraction for homosexual relationships means his ability to have progeny very unlikely indeed? The only woman he was ever to love murdered herself rather than suffer the shame of being his lover. Some will scoff, some may laugh, but to breed with relatives produces problems—perhaps problems so severe we will never be able to understand the hell that raged in Hitler's mind.

If a demon can enslave a human host by possession, why would it not be possible for Satan himself to inhabit the bodies of those willing to trade their soul for a favor? All of these despots, who have only one goal in mind—supreme dominance over the human race. This proposal for the answers as to why man's habit is prone to kill his brother will never be answered by our evolutionary friends. The answer to man's history can be only answered from the pages of the Bible. But it seems that many people are willing to take advice from pagan rock worshippers. One could guess the worship of dead things is complicated, or perhaps it is easier to renounce one's very soul and embrace the lie.

This practice is a vile testimony to the fact declaring there is no GOD while professing you possess no soul means perhaps you might be right the GOD gene is missing for some. You have described your obsession for rocks and dead things to perfection, for if there is no GOD, worshipping the dead and rocks it would seem would be a natural substitute. But a closer look at the truth reveals it is a supernatural substitute of GOD for the fork-tongued dragon.

Sounds like even though the big three may have been enemies, they all achieved the same detestable, outrageous, and common goal of trying to destroy the human race. Neanderthal logic surely not considered normal by any logic not deeply rooted in megalomania. As I have stated earlier, Neanderthal DNA is found in people of European descent and also people of Asian descent. All the big three—Hitler, Stalin, and Mao—came from regions where Neanderthal DNA can still be found.

It would appear there are many facts surrounding the origins of man. Many are simply scoffed and laughed at by the humans with no soul. The conclusions are easy to come by, and the conductor of this orchestra is easily recognized. Death and murder is a common goal, and the guy responsible is…

> The fall of Lucifer
>
> How you are fallen from heaven, O Lucifer,[a] son of the morning! How you are cut down to the ground, you who weakened the nations!
>
> For you have said in your heart: I will ascend into heaven, I will exalt my throne above the stars of God;
>
> I will also sit on the mount of the congregation, on the farthest sides of the north; I will ascend above the heights of the clouds; I will be like the Most High! (Isa. 14:12–14, NKJV)

Chapter 8

Rock Monkeys

Where could we possibly find ourselves in this maze of cultural beliefs? Do we think that we are better than the people who preceded us? More evolved? Let us look at the history of man, and a little bit into the future, perhaps we will find some interesting comparisons. It would be a fair analogy to say that despite where we find ourselves today, man—past, present, and future—has a propensity for violence. We make excuses to kill each other, and we will find the motives to do it no matter what.

We will look for any excuse as a motive to do the deed. Reasons usually revolve around cultural differences like religion, race, or the ways our enemies treat the rest of the world, or even themselves. But the real reasons are almost always because they have something we want. The list is endless—food, gold, iron, tin, oil, or as in the case of the Trojans, a single woman. It doesn't take much before greed soon turns into motivation and the killing starts.

Let's just say that killing each other just seems to be a genetic habit. It is just as predictable as the story of Cain and Abel. Some childish leader slighted at some level, or with greed, or possibly his own vanity, will pounce on his next victim. Then we set about trying to make our species extinct by killing each other. "Man" so much potential, even the farmer or gardener can produce beauty so wonderful only an enriched mind can appreciate it! The evolutionist may find the warmth of a skull or femur superior to the beauty of a single rose but at the price of a lost soul. But have we really evolved? Could it be we see ourselves better than the ancients? Perhaps we have we just found loopholes in man's endless killing spree?

Even the GOD who created us smiles in appreciation of our manipulation of his handiwork. Chimps just know they're hungry, tired, or it's time to procreate, which is the true purpose of the baculum, always! This comparison is the dilemma we find ourselves in. The comparisons when applied to chimps and man are simply both creatures share the same bodily function. Morals of right and wrong do not apply to any creature on the planet except us. Have we treated humanity better in the last thousand years? Expectations of evolvement are overshowed with the repeated struggle of survival. Man killing man while the devil himself stands urging the ignoring masses, "Let's do this."

There is an inherent danger with man, and it is this, "Once we start killing, we just can't stop until we have killed everyone that is willing to still keep fighting us." Should we be impressed because now wars are short? I mean really, nowadays wars only last ten years. We have provided new and improved war. We kill on a massive scale; money is no object. When it comes to killing, we have created so many weapons of mass destruction that we will not let the third world have them, for fear they will use them on us!

I mean, come on now, we can't let the third world have the really good toys. You know, we don't trust anyone but ourselves, to have the moral and ethical knowledge, to know when and where, it might be necessary to destroy the whole human race and the world. If it sounds like I am painting a picture of someone being childish, I can assure you I am not. A child would never entertain the thought of turning our planet into an ash heap, but the son of perdition would. Perhaps a cheap politician with Neanderthal tendencies or a megalomaniac with a chip on his shoulder just might pull the nuclear trigger. But how horrific would the motive need to be for such a decision? Let us pray to the GOD of Moses it never happens.

Evolutionists try to convince us we are evolving, but the sad truth is, a newborn baby has reached the pinnacle of evolution simply because he or she hasn't been lied to yet. An example as to the wisdom of the Bible would be its repeated demonstration of man's true nature. We are not evolving. We are the creatures we have let ourselves become. Man is either devoid of a soul with demonic possession or committed to the glory of man simple and unfettered with love and hope for all of mankind through his belief in a GOD of kindness and love.

The story of evolution is a simple one; you cannot prove GOD exists, so we will provide you with a new story. It is this, you have evolved from monkeys, and so there are no ethical or moral rules, and the value of religion is essentially worthless. Evolutionists realize this; there are genetic rules that make certain that in creating life, these rules must be maintained unaltered. It is easy to understand them, but breaking them has adverse consequences. Evolution makes life cheap because if you were not created by GOD, then there is no GOD, and His rules don't matter. Countless numbers of people have been deluded with the false belief of "nothing to see here, just move along."

Man is, and man has always been a creature of faith. Unfortunately for our species, which one do we follow? Faith is as much a part of us as the will to survive. The will to believe in something greater than himself man is left with a complex question. What should I believe? "Here is the truth, there is only one GOD!" There is a pretender to the throne, who mocks GOD by deceiving GOD's greatest creation, those that He loves, who in turn prove Satan's point by killing each other.

Let's consider the list of mockeries against GOD, death, murder, rape, torture, greed. Why? This is to prove we are, really are, after all just chimps and not worth of the intelligence GOD gave us. Has Satan proven his point? Evolutionists, some of us don't see ourselves as knuckle-dragging, bible-thumping idiots because we are not even supposed to use the word fool! But your admiration for the chimp is disconcerting at best. I find you're wondering when man lost his baculum, crude and disgusting; for the simplest of reasons, we never had one! GOD's plan for man was to conceive our progeny through love not through the lust of the baculum.

It should be noted a world without GOD leads to the death and murder of the weak, oppressed masses who struggle to stay alive until war and death are mercifully stopped. What is the secret of the elusive and non-provable fact? Evolution is just a supposition based on a theory that we have always been here since the earth cooled three billion years ago. I am not willing to surrender my faith to anyone or anything because when looking at history past, present, and future, I see no evolution in man or any creatures ever created past or present by our evolutionary pundits.

Yea, we get it. It took the elements billions of years to convert themselves to proteins, all this to create a giant protein soup. Through the miracle of chance, imagination, and really cool drawings, it just happened? This miracle goo eventually became man and of course everything else? If this sounds too much, like I found a pile of junk and the crown jewels were just lying there in that hubcap. This is because nothing occurs as a random spontaneous act of improvement. "Everything—and get this, *everything*—has an intelligent design DNA."

Explanation of "out of chaos comes order" has no comparison in the natural world, but it is a recurring theme in the world of evolution and of course, the paganism that created it. If you think this concept wrong, then how many hours do you look for your rock ancestors on your knees? If you leave a piece of fruit out on the counter, nothing gets better from there on out. It only gets worse.

Man once thought flies grew spontaneously by rotting matter until it was proven otherwise. The evolutionist expects you to believe something more outlandish than this. After all, we know flies don't evolve from trash. This conclusion was proven with the scientific method by experimentation. The truth is this, there is no proof for evolution, just supposition artwork and dead cold hard rocks.

Comets or meteors and dumb luck struck the earth, and here we are complete with a million species of different creatures. All separated by a mystery only now can we appreciate. However, it would seem everything is separated by the miracle of the universe DNA. Darwin once thought the smaller a creature was, the more simple its structure was. This is not always true. We now know the opposite is true—the smaller it is, the more complex it is. Larger amounts of information stuffed into smaller containers aren't an easy problem to

DANIEL SNUFFER

solve but poses many unseemly unanswerable questions for everyone except the GOD who created everything.

Even stars have an easily understandable structure and mechanics. DNA so far is more complex than anything understandable by the human mind. Any attempt of alteration leads to the eventual death of the manipulated. We have heard all the alternate stories, meteors smashed into the sterile earth providing proteins—the building blocks of mankind—and every living creature past, present, and future.

Wow, creation by accident. Creation by rock/meteor, creation by imagination? To the evolutionist, you need to understand the truth. Your belief is just essentially rock worship with a heavy slathering of ancestor worship. The rock has a strange recurring theme in evolution; it is responsible for everything. Comets, meteors, and asteroids created man and everything under the sun. It is just ridiculous. Let me remind you, Baal worship relied on the rock idols that littered the Baal worshipper's world. If you don't believe it, just ask a rock. Better yet, ask a good one like Lucy and then you can make up the rest.

If it is the fossilized rocks of chimps, or some protein laden meteor, now a part of the earth's magma, it was all just dumb luck and rock worship. The secret is, there is no secret here, and knowledge is power, even if it is false knowledge. We have been swindled to believe that the evolution fable is the real deal. If you're wondering what the draw here is, or if Satan really exist, perhaps now you can hear him laughing. He has replaced the majesty of GOD with the simplicity of the rock and found worshippers to swear on it! Dare I say it, are we so simple to believe it? Man is many things, but stupid isn't one of them, so deceit, lies, rocks, and artwork help to mask the real truth. GOD does not lie, but evolution struggles to stay alive long enough to find the next almost believable hoax.

Unraveling the genetic code is child's play compared to trying to manipulate it. In today's world, scientists have been working on this also, but even success in this endeavor won't make them a god. This is simply because it has been done before by someone who truly knew what he was doing. Man has managed to make spider goats through genetic engineering. Have we gone too far? Why would any-

114

one do such a thing? The answer is money! Science is manipulating the genetic code for a buck. I am certain that the love of money is the root of all evil because man has used evil to attain money. Money, it would seem, has complicated our existence both now and since the beginning of our history.

It has been scientifically and mathematically proven that the chances of man evolving based on some primordial soup is about as possible as blowing up a junkyard and finding in the rubble a complete 747 jet airliner. Random acts of creation are impossible because random acts of order don't happen. The only construct is this, out of chaos comes more chaos. The notion that out of chaos we find order is ridiculous. The truth is this, out of order comes more order. The GOD of order demands it. To disbelieve this is to state from darkness comes light; this is an impossible outcome. To state from light comes more light is reasonable, expected and biblically anticipated and a promise of the Holy Scriptures.

Everything we see and know to be true was true before we even discovered or understood it. Wake up! GOD is truth and order. Satan is chaos, and any results are not for the purposes of order but more chaos. In the laboratory, even mistakes that produce new and useable products came from careful orderly experimentation. Chaos had nothing to do with it. Every war ever fought by man only leads to another war later on. Once you realize the true nature of Satan, you will easily understand. We are not locked up with a madman but an angel gone insane.

Brother and sister, you have been deceived. Shake off the lies and realize everything about man is illustrated in detail in the pages of your Bible. We are a proud and belligerent lot. We consider ourselves special and can find a perceived evil and eradicate it, even if it exists only in our minds. The belief we are better than the ancient people that preceded us is not demonstrated by any measure. The real importance of the Bible is, it helps us to realize our weaknesses and to prevail over them all. The belief we are evolving monkeys has its own reward and not a good one when trading in your soul for counterfeit artwork, rocks (fossils), and imaginary stories you place a chasm between GOD and your inevitable outcome.

Why shouldn't we kill? Because we are not GOD! There are many things that can be repaired by man, but killing, death, and destruction are not counted among those repairable items. This is chaos. What is the antidote for it? It is order, peaceful relevance, and GOD! Can we kill our way to the prosperity and true goodness? But only if we can convince the masses there is no GOD. We can make a better world if we just kill all the bad people. Killing is grisly business, not for the weak of mind, body, or spirit. But without GOD, it is just so much more. Well, shall we say evolved? Evolution says there is no GOD, so there is no soul and so the majesty of man is lost to the killing fields of history.

The evolutionist would send you off to war thinking if I get killed, it's all over. The military sends you off with the belief if I get killed, it was for a noble cause, for which I will be rewarded in the afterlife. The real truth is this, "Thou shall not kill." So this is the dichotomy, what to believe? I am afraid I need to go with the GOD of the universe on this one. When you boil it down, man will take any chance for survival, especially when confronted with death, then the deep belief in a personal GOD sets in. If you have ever heard there are no atheists in foxholes, you would be smart to believe it, because it is true. When bullets fly and the blood splatters, atheist can recite the Lord's Prayer as good as any altar boy who ever lived, especially the altar boy's conviction.

Some people wonder if Satan exist, and some are convinced that he does. I am convinced that he does exist. This is simply because there always seems to be someone around that will prove he is alive and well. Through the actions of men and the belief out of chaos comes order, it is easy to see why some are deluded. It would be prudent to believe Satan does exist because he has provided man with a constant reminder throughout our history he is always plotting our demise. He hates us unconditionally for the simplest of reasons; like us, he is serving time on earth, forced to be locked up with the object of his hatred—the human race.

There is a truth that should not be missed here, out of chaos comes the eradication of the chaotic until only the orderly can prevail. Evil is not replaced by more and even more terror, but evil eventually kills itself. An orderly and predictable outcome is apparent through human history. You need look no further than the headlines through the history books to see the truth of it. Evil will destroy itself. It has no other purpose than to create chaos that leads to the eventual suicide of evil.

Evil always finds a way to kill us, and sometimes, we embrace the task with zeal by killing each other. It is a sad but a true indictment of mankind. We have not even surpassed the lost divinity of even the first murderer Cain. We have the gift of picking the wrong people as leaders. We should always remember any man with an agenda to kill is missing something in their character—GOD. As a species, we have followed man gods like Nero, Genghis Kahn, Hitler, Stalin, and Mao. Each time, they have proven to be very clever on their road to the hell on earth they have provided for us. They do have a master and do his bidding willingly, all this without apology and you may know them by the lies they preach to the uneducated. To make war with man is easy; to make war with GOD is folly. Man has gotten away with it so long we have forgotten even GOD's patience will one day be at an end. Will we then go to war with GOD himself to protect our right to kill? Some might find this funny and some may laugh but the truth is this. We all tremble at the fires consuming entire forest at earthquakes that knock entire cities off their foundation and Hurricanes that just blow it all away. Why? Well because it makes us feel small and the truth is we really are.

Any war ever fought by man usually has a basis that include a reason that gets told in school and then on to the next subject. The truth is much simpler than reason. Thoughts start with the egocentric idea that the world would be a better place, if some homicidal lunatic could just kill everyone believing the inevitable conclusion there is a GOD. Satan like the evolutionist hates mankind and both want revenge for laughing them off the stage. It is called megalomania and truly a basis for the fact the evolutionist like Satan has gone mad each deluded with their own self indulged folly.

The second item in the Bible offers us the story of Cain and Able and the predicted outcome of murder through jealousy. Is this not a microcosm of the genetic probability for our propensity to kill?

The Bible knows man better than anything the Evolutionist can fake in the Laboratory or illustrate in snappy fake pictures. What is the truth? It is simple we haven't evolved there is no evolution. We make terrible judgments on others and it would seem we kill. Oh if anything has evolved it would be reasons to murder, they keep getting better and better.

Oh don't get me wrong, our excuses keep getting better, more inventive more extreme, and more deadly. No matter what, if you are talking to a rock or a cell phone you're just plain killing. Technology has nothing to do with us evolving as humans, evolution it is just simply a tool an afterthought as cold as the rocks provided in museums. We are locked up with our satanic detractor running wild in this world. Satan hopes this will prove and provide us with the evidence and inevitably of evil but only in the heart of the soulless. Would it be possible to consider a world without the evil that has made all men accused guilty simply because of evils existence?

Satan hope is that at some point GOD will see it his way. Human opposition against it the divinity of Satan now provides us with a real look into the folly of the fork-tongued dragon. Like man's refusal to believe in the word of GOD we are now faced with the fact we can see firsthand why. Satan's handy work will get him into a special place for GOD will never exonerate the lie and the manipulation of man to kill each other is another transgression worthy of eternal judgment.

If you are counting on explaining away murder because of your intelligence or your ability to use a computer or a cell phone good luck. We see ourselves differently from our ancestors as the world we live in has changed. But has it really? GOD exists! Satan exist! When you realize this, the case against us and the entire human race, it is a simple one. We have not evolved so much as the thickness of the first page of Grandma's family bible. If anyone begs to differ, then read the historical record, and it isn't good!

What has happened is Neanderthal being genetically compatible but in the minority in numbers; the gene pool of the human race has driven Neanderthal back to between 2 to 4 percent. This is not evolution but simple genetics and true science. Is it any wonder that is why GOD forbids relations between relatives? Continued inbreeding could multiply the percentage of Neanderthal DNA. This outcome is completely part of Satan's plan, the doom of mankind.

We think ourselves better than the worshippers of Ammon/Baal. I mean, how could we compare ourselves to the deviates that burned children alive? We have improved this practice by pulling them apart in their mother's womb. What kind of progress is that? Shameful! The fires of Baal couldn't be happier and fully engorged with innocent flesh. The real reason all this is possible because of the notion there is no GOD. Like the concept from chaos comes more chaos, from evil comes more evil, and even the best lies require more lies.

Oh, haven't we evolved to a grand state, killing, murdering, and all for the best reasons...always! When will it stop? Computers, cell phones, cars, and televisions, those things make us feel that now we are getting somewhere. Satan must be laughing himself silly. What would anthropologists say about us a thousand years from now? We killed but only for good reasons? We made slaves of the entire human race for the benefit of the few and privileged? All this because it made some people feel better about deceiving the entire human race for money, fame, and the ideology that because there is no GOD, there are no rules!

How ugly will it be when they excavate the ruins of any museum, finding grand halls and exhibits that could be thought of as a great temple? Once inside, the most elaborate parts of the museum will be the shrines to the rock monkeys. Could we assume that while sifting through the junk, they find that we were a hostile murdering species, prone to killing each other and even our unborn children? All the consequences belonging to the improvable theory derived from evolution there is no GOD.

Now, do you still believe yourself more evolved than any story about any man or woman in the Bible? If you still do, then obviously, you haven't read the first few chapters in Genesis. Man cannot save himself, for if he could, it would be taught in the classroom. Once this new line of thinking took hold, it could save us as a species. The truth is, man corrupted himself as Adam and Eve were driven out of the garden of Eden by the judgment of GOD. Do you think Lucifer got a pass or is it possible Lucifer was punished also? Did GOD lock the corrupted up with the corruptor? If you read your Bible, you would know who the god of this earth is, and you would know his name and it isn't GOD.

History not evolution teaches the true nature of man. If you are waiting for evolutionists to explain the true nature of man, consider this, they cannot know if Australopithecus had a penis bone. If they do know, would they tell us? I think not because the truth is, this Australopithecus was just a chimp. Australopithecus was just an ordinary chimp wearing an ordinary chimp suit. Chimps were not a distant cousin, relative, precursor to modern man or anything remotely like us. Australopithecus may have a larger skull, but its presence could easily be present through interbreeding, which a common deformation is passed on to the progeny of those who practice it. To believe otherwise is to believe Lucy had human feet simply to amaze and thrill the onlooking masses. All of this while we let them shovel this lie into the mouths of our children by the bucketloads. All for the promise of no soul, no regrets, no worries, just worship the rock monkey!

In case you haven't noticed, we can turn the planet in which we live into a barren, lifeless ash heap within hours. All of that for what to prove a megalomaniac's point. Who will be left alive to tell who was right or wrong? Like the old saying, "Guns don't kill people, people kill people." The Bible never killed anyone; people kill each other and blame the Bible for it. The Bible is not a history of GOD, but the history of man, so predictable it is illustrated perfectly in every page. To read its pages is to understand its purpose, its truth, and the inevitable conclusion the truth will always win and always has.

The Bible is more than a religious book; it is a history of the actions of man. It was intended as a moral and ethical code designed to help us see ourselves as we really are. All this also proves almost six thousand years ago we were no better off and clearly, nothing has evolved since the Bible has been written. Rock worship isn't new and definitely not improved. It is ancestor worship, animal worship, and a remarkable self-delusion into the truly bazaar. Its practitioners are not even worthy to have a spirit guide to take them to the nothingness they swear exist but only by the rock of self-delusion.

Evolution goes hand in hand with atheism. If you are having a tough time with this concept, look at man's history. Psychotic murder of the masses comes from either worshipping a god who demands it (Satan), or a religion that condones it. Ammon/Baal, evolution, or atheism, does it really matter? Do you not realize you have been deceived? Let's remember the GOD with fifty names now, his name is evolution. It is time to wake up and realize we have not been deceived but allowed ourselves to be deceived by the grand creator of the lie.

Chapter 9

○

Of Mice and Men

You might think that the scientific evidence has already been laid out for Australopithecus link to modern humans, it has not. Sorry, no DNA from rock! The most elaborate studies have pointed out that while both species (humans and chimps) have similar body structure, a more precise examination lead to the true conclusion that Australopithecus (Lucy and all examples of her) are more closely related to the chimp.

The argument could be made that while both chimps and Lucy (Australopithecus) have recognizable similarities, those similarities set them apart from us. Is it possible that they are mixing apples and oranges just to fill the box of evolution? Evolutionists make their case based solely on the fact we have similar body structure. This may make evolutionists squirm a little, but the real truth is this, dissimilarities between Lucy and humans make us radically different. While the similarities between Lucy and the bonobos are very similar.

But if we came to this conclusion based solely on body structure, I have a quandary for everyone to figure out. Logic and science lay out certain rules and guidelines on what is a species or subspecies conclusively on the ability to interbreed. In the animal kingdom, there are two separate species that are atomically nearly identical. They look the same, and the bone structure is nearly identical, and the number of teeth is the same.

Based on evolutionary logic and reason let's, for the sake of argument, say that rats and mice are the same creature. I know they are not the same species, but let's try and make the argument that they are. They look similar enough to speculate at one time they had a common ancestor. The real clincher is they have been together in the same world since time eternal. They are not nor have they ever been the same creature.

Google says that rats have 223 bones, seventeen more than humans. Mice, on the other hand, have 221 bones. The similarities are so striking that you cannot even tell the difference by looking at pictures of the two different species. Even Google mixes up images for the two creatures on the Google image website. We can recognize the difference by the size, so the differences of the two different animals, like chimps and humans, have a size component. Our test subject animals are mostly identified by visual observation; this is determined by size.

For the purposes of a simple evolutionary experiment, let us say that all mice went extinct about three thousand years ago. Reasons could possibly be due to a mouse plague or excessive interbreeding. If we found mouse fossils, you could make a very strong case for rats evolving from mice. This is compounded by the fact during the time of Darwin DNA was not around to find the real truth. If science has a point to make, it would be that at one time they were related, but where are the transitional fossils to show the slow gradual change? The answer: sorry, they don't exist.

In comparison to the man-Australopithecus controversy, it is a veritable certainty that even the experts could not disprove the mouse/rat theory wrong. This would be especially difficult if it were true about the mouse extinction. But the truth is simple when you realize the facts.

Even their teeth are the same in number and structure, and the difference between the two animals is only two bones. This is even possibly less than the number of bones difference between us and Australopithecus, give or take the elusive penis bone. There are even dwarf rats, so the mechanics are possible. But they don't breed. They can't it; isn't possible. This is for the simplest of reasons, because they are not genetically compatible. We will soon find out they are not the same species and more than a certainty never were.

Speculation could even revolve around the fact; those two-bone difference may have given the rat the edge. This edge they needed desperately to survive; this over their smaller mouse counterparts. You might even think the two-bone difference made him bigger and stronger. If we take our experiment further, one could even make a case for the mouse not being extinct at all but evolving to the rat. The big problem here is, it is all a lie, constructed to show how silly evolution is.

Cars evolve, computers evolve, and cell phones evolve always into something better. People, chimps, rats, and mice don't. It's just that simple; genetic anomalies prevent it. Evolution does exist but only at the hands of GOD's most miraculous creatures, us. It is a construct even the evolutionists can understand. That is precisely the whole point for the deception; to be believable, it must be understood. Any explainable and understandable lie is still a lie, artwork or not.

A better car or cell phone is something we can easily understand. This is because we see it all the time. It is understandable, and its application is applied to anything dubbed new and improved, especially a better mouse trap, "just kidding." The point I am trying make here is this—although we can change almost anything mechanical, the evolutionist has made up a new story. This story they have concocted isn't the truth, it is a lie. They simply like it because any narrative that excludes GOD must be better, but for whom?

Almost any story that gives man a hand in his own evolution is always preferred. This is simply because it takes out the GOD element from the equation. It is even more inviting if there is money and fame in the endeavor. I mean, why not get paid to deny GOD and all of His creation.

What are the real differences? Mice have twenty pairs of chromosomes, rats have twenty-one pairs, humans have twenty-three pairs, and chimps have twenty-four pairs. Claims are that the two species (rats and mice) separated about eighty million years ago. That's a long time ago. Accordingly, the separation occurred and while similar, the two species are not related any longer, if they ever were. Let us speculate that in the time it took for mouse to change into the rat, humans could have evolved forty times from chimps to humans according to the experts, of course.

This fact is attributed to the rodent-rat mouse anomaly, favors the rodents. Apparently, rodents evolved faster than humans according to evolutionists. If this statement is true, and rats and mice started evolving eighty million years ago, then answer this, then why are we still here? Giant rats would have destroyed our species millennia ago. Competing species eradicate and kill competitors. This is a scientific fact.

If evolution is a constant, why did it happen so long ago? It didn't! The mouse, rat, humans, and chimps found biological equilibrium according to evolutionary thought, and either change is still going on very slowly or not any longer. Who knew? You will never hear of evolutionist use the mouse-rat comparison because it clearly points out that while physical characteristics are similar, similarities can be deceiving. The real truth is this, the rat is no more related to the mouse than humans are related to chimps, no matter how colorful the artwork is.

Rat behavior is to hunt, kill, and eat mice. Attempts to breed the two cannot occur naturally. The mouse ovum will not accept the rat sperm. The same is true for the rat ovum. It is completely safe to say the rat sees the mouse as a competitor and consequently a meal. There have been attempts to scientifically introduce sperm into each rat mouse ovum, but the egg withers and dies within hours and most certainly within days. The genetic roadblock is final and unaltered death occurs.

Despite differences in chromosomes, predators tend to prey on competing species. All of this despite genetic makeup or similarity in body structure. The predator rat has been observed under laboratory conditions, and the first impulse for the rat is to kill usually with a death bite to the spine. The conclusion is, although they are almost identical in appearance, behavior, and habitat, genetic differences prevent putting them in the same category and never in the same cage!

Consider the coelacanth; this ancient fish was thought to have first appeared about 360 million years ago. At one time, it was thought they went extinct sixty-five million years ago. That was until they found a live specimen in 1938. Again, the fossil record demonstrates that the coelacanth, like other species, resists change or as in the case of the coelacanth, it has dutifully resisted change for 360 million years according to evolution. This demonstrates the folly of evolution; they pick and choose the stories that might apply, but the ones that don't. Well, intelligent people don't talk about things like that!

Appearances can be very deceiving! Examples of hybrids do exist and can cloud the issue. There is a case of a wholphin; this creature has been determined to be three-fourths Atlantic bottlenose dolphin and one quarter false killer whale. Although bred in captivity, these creatures have been known to be found wild in the ocean. Apparently, hybrids either mate back and forth until they revert to their original species. Or it may be possible like the three-legged frog; they are genetically inferior and die before reproducing.

It should be remembered that new blood leads to new life. This may be GOD's way of bringing new life to their gene pool. But this has not been studied enough to be conclusive. Just a theory on my part, but prove it wrong! Why would evolutionists not want to study this well-understood anomaly? Well, because perhaps "GOD" protects dolphins from inbreeding to extinction. He does this by letting them go on the far edge of their gene pool; this would apparently be to correct their genetic transgressions of incest.

Perhaps it would never occur to evolutionists, and they would never consider. GOD protects all of His creatures, especially the dolphin. Of all of GOD's creatures, it is one of the most beautiful. Despite this, He made us in His image. Because He loved us and wanted us to flourish with hands and feet made perfectly to subdue the earth.

Physical similarity and supposition have turned to fact despite common sense. Physical similarity does not mean genetically compatible, nor does it point to evolutionary descendants based on similar physical characteristics. The mouse-rat experiment can be duplicated with other species—cats, toads, frogs, lizards, and even fish. Despite similarity, cats and dogs are too far away on the family tree to be considered related?

Despite the fact both have similar body structure, hunt in packs, and are carnivorous, they are both social animals living in packs for dogs and prides for the cats. Genetics has separated them in this way. The cat has nineteen sets of chromes and the dog an astounding thirty-nine pairs. Evolutionary logic dictates because they look similar, they are either the same creature or if they are not, at one time they were. This is played out with logic we can see in everyday life but has no basis in fact.

The Chevy is a car, so is the Buick. They have a common ancestor, the model T. All true but where did the truck come from? Obviously, the truck was the first hybrid, similar but distinctly different. The logic is short-circuited because while they have a common ancestor, the model T parts will not go into or replace parts from the other three. The origins of the three vehicles do not matter because all are constructed by man. It is a reality we see in everyday life but not demonstrated in genetics at all.

Evolution is a lie constructed to make the atheist feel better about the world in which they live, and they have a desperate drive to understand a world without GOD; in a world they don't understand and fight to control. Because of this, they have given man a critical role in his own evolution. GOD didn't do it because there is no GOD, only man. Man made himself; man pulled himself up by his bootstraps before there was a human foot to wear the proverbial boot.

The logic is so simple anyone can see it especially the enlightened, intelligent, superior evolutionist. None of this is proven in the fossil record, so with smoke and mirrors, it must be time. Yes, time did it; it is just so painfully slow you can't see it. Let us just ask the coelacanth who has resisted change four and a half times longer than the rat/mouse legacy. Like the coelacanth, something smells fishy, and it isn't a rat.

It is time and the decay that hides the evidence from us. The decay of rotting flesh, morbid corpses boiling in their own fermenting stink is hiding the truth from the creature that made itself over two million years ago, us. They are inches away from the creature that will prove it someday. Finally, one day, the hominid that will prove it all, our greatest ancestor—chimp X. Oh, chimp X will be a miraculous creature, twelve ribs on one side and thirteen on the other, wide hips and shoulder sockets pointing down, five sacral bones, and not to mention, an almost human foot to boot. Such a creature exists only in artwork and in the minds of the deceivers and the deceived!

They have looked on every continent in the world. They have traveled to the darkest jungles, explored the deepest caves, and sacrificed innumerable man hours in the pursuit of folly. GOD is hiding this creature from you in a place you will never find it. It is so deep and dark you will never find it. The real reason is obvious; they exist only in your minds. Not on any continent or jungle cave or savanna, but it exists only in your heads.

How old is the earth really? What is time really? Have the stars always been in the same position in the night sky? Have the oceans ever been dry devoid of the water that makes them oceans? The questions above are easily answered; simple really. It is simple as looking into history. The history we can see and understand with the mind we have been given to understand it. Oh, and by the way, the Bible and its literary older brother, the Torah, have spoken to the origins of man, and its truth cannot be captured in any evolutionary fairy tale.

The secret evolutionists are keeping from you and always will— man never existed until GOD gave us the mind to understand! Before that, as far as the human mind was concerned, there was only the vast emptiness of space and the hand of GOD! Every creature understands cold, hunger, thirst, and the drive to procreate. But only one has the ability to question why. Evolution is a dead end, and speculation only leads to more speculation. No light will ever come from evolution, or from the deep recesses of the dark crust of the earth. It was a lie created to deceive from the father of the lie, the deceiver himself.

There is no evolution, no evolving, and certainly, no light in the pits they have dug looking for a world devoid of GOD. They have moved mountains looking for something that isn't there and never was. They haven't found what isn't there and, in the folly, have proven themselves wrong. If they find the endeavor unfulfilling, it drives them even more. We should ask this question if evolution is fake, then is the Bible true?

If Australopithecus is a chimp, then is man a standalone creature made in the light of he who created us? We have a drive in us to understand, to seek the truth, and live with hope in a world created exclusively for us. We seek to understand the mysteries of the universe and touch the stars. Chimps don't do that and never will. They don't need to. Chimps live in a much simpler world than us, a paradise really. In a world full of food, warmth, and abundant necessities needed for a full life. They don't change simply because they are one with their world and, of course, why change? They have predators and the tools to survive them also. They will never understand us or we them. We will never be them, and they will never be us. The similarities between us stop at the ability to breathe, eat, and sleep.

There are those that claim that man has evolved to the only creature that can protect the planet in which we live. Global conferences go on for weeks on the subject. While full of atheist/evolutionary thought the haughty boastfulness and self-righteousness environmentalists forget it was GOD Himself who commanded of us to protect the planet in the first book of the Bible, Genesis. Where is the evolutionary god now? How does he feel about the great deception leaving its followers unfulfilled? Perfectly self-righteous and indulgent in the greatest lie ever told, there is no GOD.

Satan has proven like the mind of the simple chimp; some men would embrace evolution over GOD. The GOD who created the world, all species, and it would seem everything in it. Evolution provides the practitioner what they want to believe, with no guilt, easily hidden in the belief there is no GOD. Evolution, it is full of excuses, secrets, deception, and outright to lies. Penis bones are too small to survive a million years. Some chimps had human feet; we just can't find any. Baboon skulls are human, really human, and in light of all of this, GOD is hiding the proof of evolutionary evidence. It is simple really; you can't hide what doesn't exist, but you can still look for it and they do.

GOD has hidden the evidence from you in a place that never existed and in a time that never was. The rest was made up in your mind. The father of lies has done his best to help the man/monkey myth survive. He has driven you to dig in empty holes, and occasionally, you find animals perceived by you to be a protohuman. You assume there is no GOD and so the only solution left is the vast numerical impossibility of evolution. The sad truth is, you hold with contempt those who would point out you have been deceived. If telling the truth is a crime, then only the criminals benefit.

Some anthropologists have had the audacity to declare them (chimps) fake in spite of the evolutionary bullies that hide the truth with an endless string of lies, half-truths, and imaginary artwork. What they have found are chimps, fossilized rocks of a long line of chimp ancestors. Calling them human is silly because despite artwork, exhibits, and pamphlets, they are just chimps.

Inbreeding, localized habitat, and the natural world have changed them. Like the bonobos (pygmy chimp) and the chimp, they separated too long ago to interbreed anymore. They have interbred to the inevitable conclusion interbreeding has left the two chimps related no longer. Now they are no longer the same compatible creature, if they ever were. They are always just too far from humans to ever be a contender for the protohuman of the week.

We use rats and mice to conduct experiments in the lab and find the data useful. But if we find evidence in the natural world that points away from evolution, we wonder in amazement but refuse to see the facts as they are. Your fossil finds of deformed cranial subjects leads you to believe, "Alas, we have found it, man's great-grandpa," when what you have found is the deformed skull of an inbred chimp. Congratulations!

I have to give it to them though exactly how many fossilized chimps are in the basement of the museums or just left in the ground and covered so no one can see. The story of the three little pigs just isn't that good if you take the wolf out of the story. Skull deformation is a common sign of inbreeding. There are many others, but inbreeding chimps into humans just isn't rational conceivable or believable. This is the truth. They don't want you to know, kids!

You would believe it if rats and mice told you, but our closest living relatives have no lessons here and nothing to prove and certainly nothing to teach. The truth is certainly not as impressive as a fairy tale hoax and certainly not as mesmerizing as cold hard rocks that prove nothing but the ingenuity of man to find them. If you find on occasion an adult chimp skull, how tempting is it to stick it on the fossilized remains of an adolescent to provide the large skull necessary for the ancestor of all mankind to exist? Just one small problem, how did that huge head come out of a small chimp pelvis?

> Skull buried for 100,000 years at Xujiayao in the Nihewan Basin of northern China, the recovered skull pieces of an early human exhibit a now-rare congenital deformation that indicates inbreeding might well have been common among our ancestors, new research from the Chinese Academy of Sciences and Washington University in St. Louis suggests. (Source: Everding, Gary. Washington University in Saint Louis theSource. March 20, 2013)

Well, I disagree with the statement of chimps being related to humans. But I embrace the honesty of Gerry Everding's conclusion that chimps interbreed. This conclusion leads us to believe evolutionists downplay this simple fact and embrace the obvious outcome of interbreeding as natural selection, which it is not. While deformations are a common in inbred animals and humans alike, the occurrence maybe rare and more than this rarity is to find one that fits the evolutionist criteria as early human.

> Several adult females were at risk of breeding with close male relatives. Most successfully avoided close inbreeding but in one case a high-ranking male in the community mated with his mother and produced an offspring. In contrast to recent data on chimpanzees (P. t. verus) from the Taï

forest, Côte d'Ivoire, no evidence of extra-group paternity was observed in our study. Reanalysis of Taï data using a likelihood approach casts doubt on the occurrence of extra-group paternity in that community as well. (Source: Constable, Julie L., Mary V. Ashley, Jane Goodall, and Anne E. Pusey. "Noninvasive Paternity Assignment in Gombe Chimpanzees." Wiley Online Library, December 21, 2001.)

The truth of inbreeding is glairing, but in contrast, EGP (extra group paternity) means most chimps avoid sex with chimps from another group. They in turn stick to their own social group and apparently will breed among their own relatives before entertaining a union with a healthy adult male from another group. Thoughts of evolution through interbreeding may be entertained by some, but the reality is, it devastates the populations that practice it. Inbreeding as you might think is the primary cause of going extinct second only to being hunted to extinction. This is an explanation as to why chimps live in small groups, and the finding of associated fossils also as you might expect are extremely rare.

They (evolutionists) really thought they had a good thing going with Neanderthal. With genetic testing, they have proven him to be a cousin to us of sorts. But what is the real story? It is simpler than you would believe. With an open mind and the belief in history, let us figure out who Neanderthal really was. Everything we know about them gives huge clues as to their true nature. He was twice as powerful as the strongest of us. With his strength came the narcissistic drive and greed necessary to dominate everything. Where does a five-hundred-pound gorilla set? Answer: Anywhere he wants! He brought madness, disease, and even consumed the flesh of his own kind. We look on our progeny with love Neanderthal looked at each other and found something to eat. Any creature willing to consume its own kind would view everything as a meal.

He was the spawn of Satan, Nephilim; he has plagued us from the beginning. Lies, deceit, treachery, and of course, murder, the greatest detective story ever told really. How the seed of man was corrupted by the father of lies. How the strange skulls of the pharaohs were inherited from their fathers. How they believed themselves gods. When faced with the real GOD, they dwindled to insignificance. This will be coupled with how desperate genetically corrupted men sealed their fate by fighting with the enemy instead of against him. Now you know the truth not by fate or word or deeds by the common sense blown into the nostrils of our first father, Adam.

The Bible speaks of giants and men of great strength, and they do not use their power for anything good. They seek and desire of human women, which accounts for their not being any mitochondrial DNA found in any of their genetic offspring. By now, the puzzle pieces should be coming together. Evolutionists will say that I am crazy, but I am in good company because it is in the Bible/Torah. Ah, the real truth, finally science is finding out what the Bible has proclaimed since the beginning and the truth of it also.

Man has been infected by another creation, this one designed to destroy the human race. This hybrid created by human women and the fallen ones (the watchers or Nephilim) produced not only the desire to dominate, defy, and destroy the human race but brought with them disease and the intention to corrupt GOD's creation, man. No matter if Neanderthal was a wild beast or an intelligent manipulator, he has been spreading his seed throughout the human community for ages.

This anomaly was well understood in biblical times, and the pages of the Bible take note and document human interaction with them. In the end, GOD's creation was not defiled completely with Neanderthal DNA. Outnumbered, the genetically inferior Neanderthals' days were numbered. It is not a battle easily won, but when we understand that, we can refuse to accept the inevitable simply by choosing good over evil. Could it be that we control the destiny of our very own DNA? The evolutionists will say no, but I think the evidence speaks for itself.

The agnostic will claim he just doesn't know, but the atheist claims he does know, and he is pretty sure he doesn't have a soul. The real truth is, he is probably correct for either he never asked for a soul from his Creator or he asked not to have one from a god who is a liar, and he cheats and steals. Worshipping rocks and digging them up from the dark recesses of the earth will never make mice and rats cousins. The GOD's truth is, this one chromosome is a chasm too far to cross, but the divide between two is a mathematically impossibility. As you may conclude, chimps and humans divided by the two chromosomes were never the same creature...ever!

It is a fact that the genetic record shows a very great resistance for the genetic alteration of anything. The very nature of man is extremely different than the genetic disposition of almost all of GOD's other creatures. Man, it would seem, has found a very special knack to keep himself from going extinct. We can eat virtually anything and keep our species alive. We are not predisposed to be vegetarians but can survive on vegetables alone. We can survive on meat alone, but while this strategy may not be completely healthy, it may still be argued our dietary habits promote a species prone to survive. These facts are irrefutable and have a sound basis in the truth.

Chimps, gorillas, and orangutans—while primarily herbivores—do not have a survival strategy based on meat. Chimps have been observed eating meat, but its occurrence is reported to be low. However, evolutionists use this as evidence that chimps are giving us a glimpse into the first moves to becoming human. With the consumption of meat, less time was needed for foraging for vegetables, and idle time drove the chimp to use his mind to become human? This is just a theory, but its incidence makes no sense because meat consumption and enlarged brain capacity have exactly zero count and zero incidents in any other species.

The facts are glaring and help expose the ruse for what it is just a lie. If meat eating drives an enlarged brain, then it would make sense that those who have been eating meat the longest would be the smartest. Lions, tigers, and bears would beg to differ—that is, if they were smart enough to consider the question. Do we believe jargon like this? This is spouted out like it is a part of the theory but makes no sense compared to the totality of the natural world.

Make no mistake, evolution is, was, and will be a psychological propaganda with an agenda of innumerable lies. The insistence and insinuation that only stupid people believe in GOD is very clear. This points to psychological propaganda and includes repeating it often to beat down those who should know better. The reality of evolution is this; one guess is based on another until when you look at it closely you see that the fallacy begins to fall apart. A guess based on a guess is not science, and its value is basically just a guess. The facts are, evolution is just a guess based on replacing GOD with nature and if you think this is new, you couldn't be more wrong.

People of all walks of life can enter into a covenant with any religion they want. But I would suggest they express a deep personal belief in the one GOD—the GOD of Creation. For Christians and Jews, that GOD is Yahweh. In Matthew 13:24–30, we have the parable of the tares (weeds). The Bible tells the truth about our human existence. We have been infiltrated by those who seek our destruction. While the parable suggests letting the two grow together (weeds and tares), for only one type will be gathered at harvest time. Nehalem/Neanderthal with the will to be so evil that even what is left of his small genetic material still plagues us today and expresses itself with earthly demons…Hitler, Stalin, and Mao.

While being separated on the issue of the soul, it should be noted that we do have a soul and a personal relationship with Him who gave it. We know when we are being lied to. Just as digging in the ground will never find the missing link. The search for your soul is something you can find; it is attainable and findable, but you must ask the One who gives away the priceless just for the asking.

Chapter 10

○

The Ruse

It is my intention with the collections of these words to bring in to full light the evolution of evolution. Full of mystery and intrigue, and to state blatantly the facts of evolutionary theory, and most importantly, the odds it finds with itself. With each new find through evolutionary discovery, we see time and time again the dead end of wishful thinking and fantasy coupled with outright deception.

In the case of Piltdown man, he was a complete fraud right down to the stain on the human skull and orangutan jawbone. The ruse was so horrific even the evolutionists had to admit the forgery. The case of Java man is simply a case of mistaken identity. The skullcap of giant gibbon and the collection of random fossils lead us to the conclusion Mr. Java is very closely related to if not an extinct giant gibbon.

Java man was discovered near in the same strata as the Wadjak skulls. These two totally human skulls were found in the same strata with fauna (plants) very similar to Java man. This fact alone points to the probability that Java man was alive during the same time as modern humans. If he was ever alive at all, the chimp is the most probable explanation with the skullcap of a giant gibbon.

Mr. Dubois's discovery is often described as bad science. In essence, his find is either a giant gibbon or whatever a fossilized skullcap might lead to with a little imagination. Mr. Dubois was looking for "the missing link." What he found clearly poses more questions than it answers, and it always will. Without tissue or even proof of what such a creature would look like, the artwork stands alone as to what this creature might really look like. I would seriously question if it ever existed at all.

Time and time again, evolution gives man an excuse to not believe in the GOD who created everything. Their facts are flawed, as the pseudoscience of evolution leaves man in a kind of spiritual limbo, and frankly, it is not worth the time or confusion it brings the listener. The lack of transitional fossils leads us to a new question, if evolution is wrong, then could the Bible be right? That is the dividing line between evolutionists and Creationist. Both claiming each other wrong, but as science gets closer to the truth, they are catching up to GOD. Before evolution, there was GOD and so scientifically, like the alternate viewpoint, evolution touts itself as the dividing line or a theory worthy of consideration instead of a Grand Creator.

The basic genetic structures in every living creature are designed to not allow genetic change. Just as GOD blew the first of breath into Adam, He blew it into you. Now you know! We were designed not to change; just as you genetic makeup is not changeable, the Bible's claim is true. He is the unchanging and unchangeable GOD, and apparently, so are His creations.

Not being able to manipulate DNA easily, on the rare occasion, when it does occur, death and sterilization are the scientific admitted outcome and outright fact! The evolutionist has created for us the juvenilization of civilization. This complete with the dumbing down of everyone, even themselves. Science has spoken, and he is GOD, the epitome of the truth.

If you need reason to stop believing the lie, then for your edification, let's look at some forbidden science. For clarification, forbidden science is essentially unexplainable artifacts so difficult to explain they are dismissed outright even before they are discovered. Why would someone do a thing like that? The answer is simple, how about to keep those scientists who dismissed those facts gainfully employed. Imagine the empty bookshelves devoid of books in the public library. All because evolutionists won't be able to provide books from the evolutionary experts any longer. What is the real truth, and will it ever be delivered for the consumption of man? The answer is yes, and the truth has been around for a long time.

Evolution will be safe and sound as long as they are not obliged to tell the truth of evolution. The evolutionary rules and regulations that keep secrets covered in the dark. How it continues to deceive even its conceivers oftentimes by rules based solely on opinion alone and not the facts. Human and chimp fossils found in the same strata are determined by evolutionary theory that the chimp fossils are older is just silly. This opinion is based on the personal belief there is no GOD; therefore, extinct chimps evolved into as us is not very scientific, is it?

Is it possible for the bone marrow of an extinct creature to survive for seventy million years in the earth undisturbed? Apparently, it is. Archaeologists have found bone marrow in the leg bone of an extinct Tyrannosaurus rex. If you Google the subject, you will be astonished to find out that this is exactly the case. It is described as gelatinous, red, and pliable resembling in makeup the collagen of birds. This subject is taboo for the evolutionary worshippers, but it exists and has been studied in the laboratory.

> March 24, 2005. A Tyrannosaurus rex fossil has yielded what appear to be the only preserved soft tissues ever recovered from a dinosaur. Taken from a 70-million-year-old thighbone, the structures look like the blood vessels, cells, and proteins involved in bone formation. Most fossils preserve an organism's hard tissues. (Source: "T. Rex Soft Tissue Found Preserved." National Geographic. https://news.nationalgeographic.com/news/ 2005/03/0324_050324_trexsofttissue.html.)

Let us look at the above facts and put some puzzle pieces together. Neanderthal DNA is found in the teeth of our extinct cousins. Neanderthal died out some thirty thousand years ago according to the experts. Time has reduced his DNA to where it can only be unlocked from the protective enamel from nerves in his teeth. The enamel in the teeth provides almost a time capsule preserved in what would be a glass time vault.

Tyrannosaurs rex died seventy million years ago, and his DNA can be retrieved from a leg bone buried in the ground. This is not a question but a scientific fact. Absent of suppositions or theory, the facts are the bone marrow exist! The reason given is that because T. rex had a diet rich in iron. This has locked in the DNA by a process similar to the known method of formaldehyde preservation. But even formaldehyde preservation has its limits; I mean, come on now seventy million years!

The preservation of soft tissue with formaldehyde gives out in less than a hundred years. We have all seen the broken-down exhibits in the science lab where soft tissue is coming apart with the cloudy results, making the item on display a gooey mess. This explanation is obviously for the mentally weak, the stupid masses they think they are speaking down to. Who are they to tell us what to believe? They have not been able to prove what they believe nor do they intend to!

Despite the bullheaded defiance, an intellectual roadblock exists, making the pursuit of the truth a taboo in evolutionary thought. The miracle of DNA is rapidly proving the evolutionary theory a figment of the imagination of the dumbed down few and getting fewer. The obvious question will arise if you ask, did not Neanderthals have a diet rich in animal protein? Science says yes, and they should have had loads of iron in their bodies to protect their bone marrow also. Shouldn't this have protected that bone marrow locked in their bones? But sadly, it is now only found in their teeth... Sure?

So now, what theory can we come up with to explain such an anomaly? How about we come up with a theory that says the older an extinct creature is, the less likely you are to obtain viable genetic material from such a creature. Common sense, right? But not to the experts! Now, this new theory makes common sense. Let us call this the common sense theory. This is because practicable observation leads us to this conclusion. The genetic code is preserved better in last week's roadkill than the first creature ever killed by the model T. Such a simple concept a child could understand it.

Let's take our new theory one step further. Common sense theory should shout out that the DNA in the T. rex is better preserved because he died more recently than Neanderthal? What? Wait a minute, this new theory makes sense. But what do the experts say about it? Sadly, they don't say much, mostly because there's nothing to say except they are sorry. With evolutionary theory, we find common sense is not that common and seldom makes sense.

Is it easier to conclude that an animal through pure chance made chemicals in its fossilized bones that surpass logical explanation? Or possibly, the experts were wrong and wrong and wrong again. How wrong? Wrong enough to dupe the public they so continuously looked down on completely. This is possibly because if we are dumb enough to believe their rhetoric, we don't get extra credit for IQ points. All the while, they ridicule us for a manifest belief in the GOD who did it all.

Let us consider that something is very, very wrong here. Have we been so dumbed down that we are ready to consider the ridiculous as fact and fact as ridiculous? Please! They are so mentally clouded by a hope in the silliness of evolution; desperation is settling in big time. Evolutionists are starting to look toward the truly bizarre for a logical explanation. All this is just a little more wrong than that. It is truly sad.

With this impossibility firmly undeniable is the Bible is starting to make scene. This is especially evident if you consider that the finding of bone marrow in extinct dinosaurs is not a one-time event. Some estimates conclude this chemical preservation has been found in fossilized bones dating back two hundred million years. Really! Is this preservation process so complex the mind of Homo sapiens cannot comprehend it, duplicate it, or intelligently explain it?

The collagen in the T. rex is exactly where it should be, located in the porous bones of the animal subject. Porous means a lot of holes where the elements could destroy its structure. Now Neanderthal, on the other hand, his DNA is found only beneath the enamel of his teeth. This is extreme conjecture if you do the math. T. rex has been dead 2,300 times longer than Neanderthal or so that is what they are asking you to believe. Come on, how stupid do they really think we are?

Bones and sponges are porous, and the enamel of the teeth is like glass protecting its contents for thousands of years. Something is wrong here, and it doesn't make logical sense. It was discussed earlier that children are disappointed when they find that man and dinosaurs were never alive at the same time. But make no mistake about it. There are discoveries that make the Flintstones look like an award-winning documentary film.

Some reports claim that for the last five hundred years, they have been finding stones around the Nazca desert in Peru. These stones are called the Ica stones, and they were first found by Catholic missionaries in the 1500s. These stones are carved with the daily routine of the Nazca people. The depiction of the daily activities of the Nazca people are striking and found enshrined in cave tombs. If you google Ica stones, you will find beautiful carved stones complete with anatomically correct dinosaurs. Yes, I said it because it is true!

The pictures, while beautiful, also show people riding on dinosaurs and even being eaten by them. They are certainly not fakes considering they have been finding them for hundreds of years. These stones have been verified by experts as ancient; this is because the patina on the stones could not be faked. Why would anyone fake a picture five hundred years ago to give evolutionists a black eye four hundred years before it was even invented? Silliness!

Do you, evolutionist, want to give up now or don't you realize at this point you yourselves have been deceived by the devil himself. The GOD of all things whispers in the blowing wind you have been deceived by an improbable absurdity coupled with the imagination to make it appear to look true. The beauty of the truth is, it will always be the truth. The fallacy of evolution has disproved itself many times. Every new evolutionary discovery has eventually played itself out into the fraudulent hope it really is.

Like a fossil, because it is a rock, it cannot be accurately dated. The Ica stones are considered ancient and attempts to declare them a fraud is difficult at best, largely because there are over fifteen thousand of them, and they have been finding them since 1960.

The main proponent associated with the Ica Stones is the late Dr. Javier Cabrera (deceased 2001) who is credited with popularizing the stones as well as displaying and caring for them in the museum that was contained within his house in Ica. Cabrera termed these stones "gliptoliths" and posited that they were created by "Gliptolithic Man" who came to Earth from the Pleiades. He first came upon the infamous stones when he was given one for his birthday in the early 1960s. The beautiful stone interested him and he was able to buy more from a farmer in the region. The farmer brought Cabrera more and more stones but would not reveal how he was making them, eventually leading Cabrera to become convinced of the authenticity of the stones. (Source: http://pseudoarchaeology.org/b03-ross.html)

Mr. Dawson could only produce one Piltdown man skull in his lifetime. Could the people of Peru produce on an industrial scale over fifteen thousand frauds? The discovery of Mr. Dawson (Piltdown man) while an embarrassment to the evolutionary community is, was, and still remains a fraud.

There are no evolved creatures, only extinct ones. It is pretty plain to see if you are ready to open your mind to the facts. Extinct creatures didn't evolve into anything because they are extinct! If they had survived on the scale, evolution expects to further their species. This would lead to literally so many fossils they would be stored in a warehouses, and we would be kicking them out of the way on nature walks.

Homo sapiens have now evolved to Homo sapien sapiens, all of this in my lifetime. Did we really evolve that much in the last fifty years? Oh yes. Is it because of computers? How about because of cell phones? It is ridiculous hype intended to get you to go along by pandering to your sense of intelligence or lack thereof. Why would anyone do such a thing? I mean, is there any reason why the public is continuously duped with this colorful and at times artfully done ruse? Yes, and we will see why. Stay tuned and get ready for the ruse has exposed itself.

It is as simple as this, if anyone can get you to believe a lie, they can get you to believe anything. Why? It is about controlling your mind. It is about controlling the masses. It is about controlling the public. It is about controlling anyone with an original thought. It is instilling in everyone the belief that those with the brains should be making the decisions. That's okay until those decisions have a negative impact on the people faced with the repercussions of those decisions.

The powers that be make great institutions dedicated to tell you what to think—libraries, museums, schools, teachers, students, everyone, everywhere. They create what they would like you to believe is that what is in your best interest. Global warming is not what you would think. No one intends on controlling our climate. They are pretending to care about the deteriorating condition of the climate, but it is not true. I hate to tell them, but climate changes! The idea is to get you to believe that they care so the pollution never stops. Bait and switch, the people who pretend to care will make billions. They have convinced themselves recognizing it is doing something while nothing is being done about it because the money profit just isn't there. So let us just keep polluting its good business for the profits for the Fortune 500.

They will spend billions looking for solutions to problems they either cannot stop or will never stop. For the simplest of reasons, it makes money for them or the people that pull their strings. After all, they are the ones doing the polluting. You're being poisoned, and they want you to pay for it. Can you see now that Neanderthal never went extinct, he never went anywhere? He is full of himself; he has tricked you into being complicit in your own demise. That is nothing compared to the fact that the greed of others is killing us, and they have found a way to profit from it. There is a plastic pile in the Pacific Ocean as large as the State of Texas and it's getting bigger. There is no profit to be gained by removing it and so it continues to grow. Like evolution, there are somethings we would rather not talk about.

Autism is out of control and climbing, but you are constantly reminded to get your children vaccinated. Pharmaceutical companies lobby Congress for exemptions from lawsuits over shoddy products. All the while, they constantly remind us to put their trash into our bloodstreams. Is it pollution or pharmaceutical use? Does it matter as long as the plastic pile grows? Your child's condition isn't any concern of theirs. After all, they have made their money, and now it's your problem. Kindness and concern are only a characteristic they reserve for themselves, and the profit margins grow. How could people be so cruel it's easy when you have no soul.

The power of money has brought about a great truth, one that they don't want you to know! They control everything. They have what is truly the brotherhood of the buck. Keeping you sick and stupid makes money. Having you believe that some in the government care about you makes money. Isn't it clear by now there is nothing you can do about it because you gave away all of your power at the last election? My belief has a very notable outcome the caveat of truth a lie is never rewarded, but the truth always is. The plotting against GOD's creation over the profit of the corporations has a reward, and they will not like it.

Ah, but there is one catch, guess what it is? GOD! This is why there can't be a GOD, not anyone to see the evil in their hearts. Especially when the system they have so cleverly constructed finds that all paths lead to your wallet! When the GOD of creation asks you, "Cain, where is your brother?" Ah, evolution. That's the answer. No GOD, no creation, no Bible, no truth except money is the root of all that is good. Again, I ask, "Cain, where is your brother?"

Treaties, limits, exemptions, they are all a farce and not to mention who will pay for it all. The world is a polluted place and getting more polluted all the time. What is the real aim of climate control? The answer is simple. They intend to bilk trillions of dollars from every man, woman, and child in the world for the pursuit of greed and wealth. Who will benefit while the world spirals out of control and your children are left to roll around in industrial filth?

Hear this well and you would benefit from this bit of information; every problem they create for us makes money for them. Cain killed for jealousy and now they kill for greed. Where is your evolved Homo sapien now? War-killing weapons designed to kill for profit the billions into the coffers of those who have sold their soul to the devil. All of this for the wealth that will lead to a dead end; no salvation, no redemption, just a one-way ticket out of the human race. Ah, globalism—the answer to all questions the globalist seeks, even if it's just a lie that will be paid for with their souls when GOD demands payment for the harm done to his people.

Wake up, don't you realize that if it makes money, it is legal? If putting aluminum in jet fuel makes money, do you think they wouldn't do it? Pumping billions of nanoparticles of aluminum into the lungs of citizens is good for business. "What business benefit?" you may ask. The answer is more shocking than you might think. All of these companies pharmaceuticals, hospitals, doctors, lawyers, the oil industry, the airlines, the government…everyone. When will it end? The answer is when the GOD of Abraham, Isaac, and Jacob puts an end to it, and so he will.

With the delusional power of wealth comes justification for horrendous act against of destruction of the planet. Airlines travel to populated areas. Nanoparticle aluminum brings rain to population centers and, of course, metal toxicity, sickness, and death. Oh well, the price of progress is a slippery slope, not for the weak or weary, best suited for the strong, powerful, and the globalist who just has no soul. After all, the ones best suited to live in the world they have created are them, and they demand we pay for it all.

Disease and sickness are the result; the manipulation of your genetic welfare is nothing because the greed of man has no con-science when it comes to the sacred act of making a buck. Greed has no empathy or sympathy for the fallout they create when they pollute the world. They would like you to believe you have a say in it. They rely on your stupidity, your ignorance, your reluctance to demand change. After all, they are superior, they are smart, and they are in control. The control they seek leaves out one important truth! Soon GOD will remove their tyranny and replace it with a reward held solely for those with no soul.

But are they really in control? Sadly, they are not in control of anything that can exempt them from what they have knowingly done to GOD's creation. No amount of pollution can save them from the world they have created for us. There is no "get out of jail" card free here. They have created evolution so that they can sleep at night all the while damning themselves for an eternity.

Evolution has done more to destroy the moral and ethical path to perfection than any fraud ever conceived of or thrown on the human race. But let's not forget, it has made many people wealthy. But there is a price to be paid, and it is the disease created from your money machines that will infect you also. But alas for you, there is no GOD, no salvation, no redemption, no hope, and no turning back. But maybe, just maybe, it can be stopped by truly repentant people who by the grace of GOD might find their souls again and honestly pray that it stops.

Perhaps it never occurred to them they have caused the manipulation of their own DNA. The narcissism, the loathing of everything intended to be pure, and clean all lost for them when they traded their soul for money. The saying I think is, "GOD helps those that helps themselves," but for the Neanderthal mind, it is, "I help myself by helping myself; therefore, I must be a god."

Like the criminals having genetic anomalies that predispose them to a life of crime. Perhaps when science identifies the soul gene, it will be found it just isn't there in our Neanderthal counterparts. Was it traded away, or did they just lose it, or could it be just plain belonging to someone else?

Not all leaders are bad. Some are destined to greatness, for GOD hears the cries of His people. While the cries of "Help us!" echo in the halls of heaven, he sees us, and he cares, and he acts. If He gave you such a leader, would you recognize him? If he came from nowhere and against incredible odds was given to the power to lead, would you follow? If he told you he loved your country and he loved you, would you believe? If he found you a job, would you believe? If he cut your taxes, could he be your friend? Now consider this, would you choose not to follow him because he was called a liar by those who have been exposed as liars themselves?

The liar has only one master and so is a slave to the lie, and the father of all lie's the devil himself. If they must lie to have power, where does their power come from? Where is the soul of a man who lies to deceive? The answer is easy—he doesn't have a soul, and his heart is vacant. What is the saddest of all is the state of affairs of those who cannot see that the plot of evil against good is being played out on a stage before your very eyes and half of you just don't care.

Satan is the father of lies. He has no hold on anyone or anything simply because when you come to realize what you have done wrong and ask for forgiveness, his bonds are broken. If he has your soul, he gained it through a lie. Has the intelligence of our superior handlers forgotten? Fraud has always been acknowledged as a legal clause to abolish any contract. The fraud of evolution finds the evolutionist without a soul and a broken contract with GOD.

No power under the sun can take away your soul, for you have free will! Use it; free yourself, free your soul for there will be a time when it will be too late. Free will is useless if you have imprisoned your soul to hell where the lie is truth and the truth is a lie! But you can break out! I am not GOD. I don't pretend to know his will for you or what judgment that may lay ahead for anyone. Like the military saying, "It is above my pay grade." I cannot pass judgment, nor do I have the intellect to comprehend the case against anyone or anything. I have not lived your life and have no idea of the perplexities of your life but you do! Ask for hope, ask for guidance, and if it's not too late, have the dignity to ask for a soul, and he will give you one. If He can heal the sick, make the blind see, and turn water into wine, perhaps His greatest miracle of all would be to give you a soul and so He can.

When asked by GOD, "What did you do for me?" The best answer will be, I looked for the truth and found you! The wrong answer will be, I looked for wealth and found it. But, GOD, I seemed to have misplaced my soul because it just isn't here. Death and taxes are sure, but riches beyond the grave are not, just ask Rockefeller; his wealth cannot buy him a soul or anyone else either. It bought him a record, seven heart transplants, and he lived to be 101, and hopefully in the end, found a soul.

Imaginary enemies do exist, and following this concept will create an enemy of everyone. Thou shall not kill, but it sure makes those weapon stock prices soar. Thou shall not steal, but if you can lobby

Congress to make it legal, I'm sure I could get rich. Thou shall not commit adultery, but trading in for a new wife is okay, isn't it? That is the problem; your free will is used to destroy the will of others when it is based on lies and deception. GOD is the only obstacle getting in the way of your success. Why can't I just do what I want? You can but breaking man's covenant with GOD will not work for you forever, and you lose the sight of that, which is most important. Do I have a soul?

Time for GOD is like looking at a string he can look at either end, both ends, and everything in between. To say there is no GOD leads to a complex question. Is it better for men to say there is no GOD or is it worse for GOD to say sorry there just isn't any you? The answer might possibly be the same for both statements, for in reality perhaps, the refusal to admit a power greater than your own identifies a person without a soul, under judgment through the divinity of GOD.

Remember this, there is an important lesson to be learned here. Joseph Goebbels and his mentor Adolph Hitler liked to use a Nazi popular saying, "If you repeat a lie and lie often enough, people will believe it, and you will even come to believe it yourself." This is known as psychological propaganda or (the Great Lie), and if you have a hard time understanding this, then consider this, it is written in Adolph Hitler's only published book *Mein Kompf*.

It is a fact that the genetic record shows a very great resistance for the genetic alteration of anything. The very nature of man is extremely different than the genetic disposition of almost all of GOD's other creatures. Man, it would seem, has found a very special knack to keep himself from going extinct. We can eat virtually anything and keep our species alive. We are not predisposed to be vegetarians but can survive on vegetables alone. We can survive on meat alone, but while this strategy may not be completely healthy, it may still be argued our dietary habits promote a species prone to survive. These facts are irrefutable and have a sound basis in the truth.

Chapter 11

○

The Bible History of Truth

For those that have said there is no GOD, you should also admit there is no soul, for one truth must lead to another and so on and so forth. It is the way of science; it is the way of truth. This is the truth we all seek, and it should be lasting and forever, a concept detailed in every creature ever created by the GOD some dismiss. And so in the dismissing, you leave yourselves defenseless in manners of the spirit and the way of the light. For some, no explanation will do, and no explanation will enlighten or produce the truth of this in their minds. For the unfortunate evolutionists, they have hidden the truth between the lies, loopholes, and missing reality they will never find in rocks.

On the subject of predictability, how does the Bible stack up to evolution? It would be senseless to compare the two, for I have laid out the subject of evolution very clearly in the pages contained herein. What does the Bible offer up as predictable enumerable and an experiment that will soon be over? History told in advance should be a valuable tool to figure out which is a pillar of light or darkness gleaned from dark holes that yield nothing but stone.

Nebuchadnezzar, the pagan Babylonian king, had a dream that laid out every kingdom ever to exist from his time until now. His kingdom was the head of gold in Nebuchadnezzar's dream the first kingdom. Daniel predicted the kingdom of Media/Persia, the two arms of silver represents a coalition of two empires that made up the empire. Incidentally, all taxes in Media/Persia were paid in silver. As silver is inferior to gold, the Media/Persian Empire represented a coalition of two and so is inferior to the Babylonian Empire ruled by one king.

Daniel went on to predict the Kingdom of Greece. The thighs were of bronze. This is a material identified with Greek weapons and especially their armor. Without bronze, Greece would have never ventured beyond its own borders. Daniel predicted through his own vision the demise of the Media/Persian Empire. Daniel saw this empire as a ram with two horns (each horn representing the two kingdoms). This kingdom was destroyed by the he-goat with one horn in the middle of his forehead.

Media/Persia ended in 331 BC at the hands of a twenty-two-year-old Alexander the Great from Macedonia, Greece. The interpretation of this vision was given to Daniel by the archangel Gabriel. Alexander the Great (the he-goat) in the book of Daniel; his historical facts are explained in detail in the pages of Daniel. The Greeks swept across Asia like in Daniel's prophesy as if the feet of the he-goat never touched the ground. It took Alexander eleven years to conquer what at that time as the entire known world.

Many depictions of Alexander show him with the horn of a goat, a depiction he apparently had no problem with for his likeness was on the Greek coins of the era. The head is usually a side view, and only one horn is visible on pictures and coins in circulation in the times of Alexander the Great. Did GOD show those coins to Daniel, or was it the luckiest guess in the history of mankind? What is miraculous about this prediction is, Daniel gave it over 220 years before it actually happened.

When Alexander visited the temple in Jerusalem, the holy men showed him Daniel's book about Alexander and his conquest. When Alexander heard Daniel's prophecies, he needed to look no further than the bronze armor on his body and silver coins he paid his solders with to know the truth of it. Alexander proclaimed the Hebrew people "the people of the book." He also declared that no harm should come to them under penalty of death. Speculation is not a just measuring stick as Alexander had seen what the temple priest had to offer and was likewise very impressed.

This, for atheists, is explained away as what they call a coincidence or just dumb luck. Daniel went on to say that the one horn on the he-goat Alexander would be broken into four horns. This did happen as when Alexander died, his kingdom split into four kingdoms. These facts again are easily explained away as coincidence by the folks with no soul.

Rome was predicted by Daniel as the legs of iron and in the time of Rome, it was described by contemporaries of the day as the iron monarchy of Rome. Iron was the main component in the steel Gladius, the sword used by the Roman soldiers that wielded them. Rome, like iron, was hard and enduring; the empire lasted fifteen hundred years.

When the Roman Empire fell in AD 476 at the hands of Barbarian tribes, it was separated into ten different segments, this corresponding to the feet with ten toes of iron and clay. This is irrefutable evidence of a GOD who inspired the prophets of that day, and the story is provided for in the pages of modern history books. Daniel made many prophecies later proven to be true, and the facts are an outright historical fact and in the pages of the good old family Bible.

Unlike the haphazard circumstances of evolution, the Bible has as many evidences in the form of corroborative evidence and therefore fact. Corroborative meaning more than one source; it is becoming more evident as the times of the ancients reveal this truth, "The Bible is true." Just as iron and clay will not mix, no better explanation or description could be given for the history of the European nations. They are constantly divided sometimes by war and sometimes by national prejudice. Europe has never been able to join together neither by consent nor by force. But to think this plan will never be attempted again is on the whole ridiculous…have you never heard of the European Union?

Napoleon considered himself the Alexander of his day, but subzero weather stopped him in Russia and later at the hands of a coalition of European States led by England's General Wellington at Waterloo. General Wilhelm of Germany made a similar attempt in WWI. This was followed by Adolf Hitler only twenty-one years later in his attack on Poland in 1939.

Attempts by nonbelievers to discredit the writings of Daniel are fruitless as the discovery of the Dead Sea Scrolls proves the content and the dates in which they are written. These dates not only are accurate, but as corroborative evidence, they prove the Bible to be true. Attempts in proving the Bible is false in teaching a flat earth are met with passages from the prophet Isaiah.

"It is he that sitteth upon the *circle of the earth*, and the inhabitants thereof are as grasshoppers; that stretcheth out the heavens as a curtain, and spreadeth them out as a tent to dwell in" (Isa. 40:22, KJV; emphasis mine).

We all know that Pythagoras, the Greek philosopher and mathematician, was the first to discover that the earth was round. This is curricula taught in public schools and private alike. We also know now that Columbus never discovered the New World Americas, but the Norseman Leif Erikson did. But the real truth is a little more disturbing than you would think. The prophet Isaiah lived in 800 BC, a full three hundred years before Pythagoras did, but according to the experts, this answer is not acceptable not only by religious oppression but also by a critical belief how could GOD and his prophets be right!

We can have some fun with this one. Pythagoras, being a scientist, has favored voting by the scientific community so his claim is preferred, so it is scientific fact; Pythagoras is the first to discover the earth is round. Isaiah, on the other hand, cheated because it was just an extremely lucky guess, or could it be because Isaiah was simply told so by GOD. This again is cheating, or could it be because GOD took Isaiah to a high enough place to see it for himself. This again would be cheating in the eyes of learned. The absolute worst answer for the scientific community would be GOD discovered the earth was round when he conceived the foundation of the earth and laid it out among the stars for us all to see in its natural splendor and beauty.

As it is easily demonstrated, science oftentimes tells you what to believe. This is because some scientists have an ulterior motive. It is a simple goal really. They want to tell you what to believe and the more you listen, the more you are conditioned to believe. It is simply a matter of accepting an input by a source preferred by the teachers of the masses. But I am old-fashioned and prefer to believe perhaps Pythagoras heard the concept from Isaiah. After all, the word of Isaiah had been around for three hundred years before Pythagoras solved his first math problem.

Columbus did not discover America because he was a bad man. The true history of Columbus was hidden until it could no longer be held back, and so now that we know his brutal history, his title has been removed. Did it work? Well, you tell me. Did you complain? Pythagoras as we all know gets the title for discovering the earth was round because science just likes a story from a scientist better. They prefer an educated pagan over a Hebrew prophet of GOD responsible for an entire book in the Holy Bible.

If evolution were proven (good luck), Charles Darwin would receive the credit for it. This would become Darwin's Law. This is because Darwin's theory would be proven, and he would get the credit not the scientist that proved it as fact. But Isaiah declared it boldly, but as science just has no room for religious belief. If the world is indeed round, it should be Isaiah's Law (the earth is round), not Pythagoras Law.

I would like to take the time to point out that evolution, while essentially just an experiment, is used to convey an alternate viewpoint to the story of creation. If this is a measure to contradict the Bible, it has failed and most notably miscrably. Like truth or lie, if one is a lie, then the other is the truth, and so I give you the history of man complete and in full contained in the pages of the Holy Bible.

The Sumerian archaic (pre-cuneiform) writing and the Egyptian hieroglyphs are generally considered the earliest true writing systems, both emerging out of their ancestral proto-literate symbol systems from 3400–3100 BC, with earliest coherent texts from about 2600 BC. (Source: History of writing. Wikipedia.)

It is a fact that the earliest forms of writing are approximately six thousand years old, and we are left to believe that man existed for 194,000 years before the thought of a birthday card entered the modern human mind. Eve is the dividing line, as she is credited with being the first modern human and essentially, the only human woman who survived to be the mother of us all. But is it possible the math could be incorrect for the 194,000 years?

> August 18, 2010. Age confirmed for "Eve," Mother of All Humans. A maternal ancestor to all living humans called mitochondrial Eve likely lived about 200,000 years ago, at roughly the same time anatomically modern humans are believed to have emerged, a new review study confirms. The results are based on analyses of mitochondrial DNA. (Source: Harrub, Brad, and Bert Thompson. "The Demise of Mitochondrial Eve.")

It is interesting to note that the age of Eve is based on mutations in the female mtDNA. They are expected to be found roughly every thousand years, but better science has found that these rates are under exaggerated and occur randomly with the incidents being much more than expected due to the father also expressing through his offspring mutated genes from his mother also and so what is the real truth.

> Regardless of the cause, evolutionists are most concerned about the effect of a faster mutation rate. For example, researchers have calculated that "mitochondrial Eve"—the woman whose mtDNA was ancestral to that in all living people—lived 100,000 to 200,000 years ago in

Africa. Using the new clock, she would be a mere
6,000 years old (1998: 279:29, emphasis added).
(Source: Harrub, Brad, and Bert Thompson.
"The Demise of Mitochondrial Eve." https://
www.trueorigin.org/mitochondrialeve01.php.)

Writing and the study of mtDNA have pointed to six thousand years of the human experience, not the 200,000 years as anticipated by the folks with no soul. Brothers and sisters, you have been
deceived, why would the evolutionist push the numbers back so far?
It is obvious to get you not to believe the truth there is a GOD!
Through truth and science evolution, your king has no clothes! Is
science throwing evolution out by the simplest form available, the
truth?

In the late 1990s, Columbia University geologists
William Ryan and Walter Pitman proposed that
a great flood in the Middle East resulted from
rising water levels at the end of the last Ice Age
about 7,000 years ago. At that time, the Black
Sea was a freshwater lake and the lands around
it were farmlands. When the European glaciers
melted, the Mediterranean Sea overflowed with a
force 200 times greater than that of Niagara Falls,
converting the Black Sea from fresh to saltwater
and flooding the area. (Source: Trimarchi, Maria.
"Was There Really a Great Flood?" National
Geographic.)

While this theory is still being reviewed, Bruce
Masse, an environmental archaeologist at Los
Alamos National Laboratory, put forth his own
theory about the great flood. He hypothesizes
that more comets and meteors than we know
have hit Earth throughout its history. He believes
the seeds of great flood stories may have sprouted

when a comet hit our planet about 5,000 years ago. (Source: Trimarchi, Maria. "Was There Really a Great Flood?")

Masse's theory derives from clues in cultural flood myths, including ancient petroglyphs, drawings and historical records, but it's the physical evidence he's after to make the case. Since Masse presented his idea in 2004, he's found support in the geological community. (Source: Trimarchi, Maria. "Was There Really a Great Flood?" http://science.howstuffworks.com/nature/climate-weather/storms/great-flood1.htm)

It would appear that while corroborative evidence for evolution is scanty at best and nonexistent at least real science is squeezing evolution out of the picture. As I have explained, real science is accomplished through corroborative evidence. An example would be two scientists preforming similar experiments producing the same results; this is a good example of corroborative evidence. Two archaeologists finding chimp bones in different parts of the world only serves to prove chimps get around. (Source: http://science.howstuffworks.com/nature/climate-weather/storms/great-flood1.htm)

It is simple to see that while science supported evolution in the beginning as early as 1990, that support began to slip until seven thousand years was introduced as a possible scenario for the great flood. The seven-thousand years number has been reduced to five thousand years only fourteen years later, as science is beginning to catch up to GOD. If you are surprised, you shouldn't be as science is in the search for truth, and the truth is GOD! As you would expect, science gets better as we begin to learn more. But evolution is begin-

156

ning to lose ground, and the chimps are getting harder to find. The five thousand years figure is extremely troublesome for evolutionists for a very simple reason—that is the time frame that totally corroborates the Bible.

Chapter 12

○

GOD is in His Word

While delving into the story of evolution, it is time to find the real story of man, the complexities of human development, and the real truth. Where did we come from, and where are we are going? The answer is long overdue and has always been available to those who seek the truth.

GOD does not speak in riddles, poems, or words not intended to make you think. Yes, you! Think! The world is distracting; everything is a distraction. Do you feel distracted? That's because you are. GOD is not up for debate, for man has been debating GOD ever since we have had the mind to question the simple but most complex word ever uttered. Why?

We love eternally, even at the loss of a loved one. We feel cheated because and after all, how will we still love them? Your love was not wasted, you have been distracted. When you realize out of your distracted state the loss, how will you fill it? When you share that love with other mourners and even strangers, healing enters in. This is for the simplest of reasons—GOD promised it, and GOD is in His word.

The love we have must be shared given freely unrestrained and full force, for it is our true destiny to share that what was given freely to us. Make no mistake, GOD loves us. How could He not. He made us in his image! Did we never consider that the GOD who loves us has given us all that we ask? Did not GOD see that man was lonely? Did He not create for us the most beautiful creature to sustain us in our loneliness?

Did not the GOD of our fathers know the loneliness in us for He himself was lonely? That is why he created us in the first place! Know the truth and find GOD! Oh, silly man, we see love, truth, kindness, and question why? Because GOD put it in each and every one of us and that is why! We go through life distracted, blind to the real issues of life. Who am I? The answer to creation is I AM. I Am that I Am! GOD is with you always if you want Him to be, but if you don't want Him, then revel in your own blindness, but remember, this GOD gives men souls; man gives evolution an extremely poor choice for the lie can't even save itself.

You should know every incident of love, loss, kindness, and our reaction to it is inspired by Him that first blew the breath of life in Adam. GOD is not hiding from you; you are hiding from him. Distraction, deception, evolution, flawed science, and now the final insult, "there is no GOD." For those who say it, I am blessed with the knowledge that my GOD is not like you, for if He was, we would all end up as stone relics in museums.

Those of you who have made a god of rocks, have your fill. Teach each other how man was created out of creatures that never needed our help in the first place. Make up endless stories, print art-work, and feel proud you have proven Satan right at least about you. That man has created a god out of rocks just so he can do what he wants, and now you know the simple truth!

GOD's creation is illustrated perfectly in the pages of the Bible. Evolution is flawed completely. We don't seek power or glory, money or fame. We are satisfied with this simple truth. "There is a GOD," and He lives in our hearts. There is no temple that can contain Him, and the only temple He wants is you. Know this, no matter what stage of life you are in—sad, happy, depressed, or just lonely—you are loved. No one is like you, and you will always have a unique gift, something special GOD wants and finds special about you.

Man was created first in the creation story because genetics dictates there must first be an XY chromosome before there can be an

XX. For the GOD of our fathers split off the Y chromosome and added an X in its place to create woman. I suppose Moses just made a lucky guess, or perhaps GOD gave him a lesson in genetics, and now you know the truth. If this sound miraculous, then considers this, GOD did it for every species that ever existed on the planet.

In splicing the XY to an XX in humans, this was his final masterpiece. For according to the Bible, Eve was his last creation. Every man can appreciate the beauty of our women. But many of us thank the GOD of creation for it. Evolutionists, now you know why we don't buy in. It is certain that woman was GOD's last creation on earth. This is true, and GOD truly outdid himself on this one. All other creatures pale in comparison to the words mother, daughter, sister, and wife. When we think of love, kindness, and devotion, we have our mothers to illustrate for us all of these concepts, and the truth of it all, we are loved.

Adam had a choice; he could have refused Eve's forbidden fruit. He could have asked GOD for another woman, but alas, he loved this one—bones of his bones, flesh of his flesh. It is the most romantic love story ever told, from the creation of man to the end of creation. How man gave up an eternal paradise for the love of his wife. GOD separated himself from us but even in that separation, He never stopped loving us. How could He stop? Like Eve, we were created for a purpose, and in your heart, you know what that purpose is—to love and to be loved!

Could we imagine GOD's heartbreak at Adam's decision to take the punishment of death with his wife? Better still, can we realize his elation over the fact He created a creature that like GOD, "we had the capacity to love?" GOD truly outdid himself by creating us for He made us like himself, perfect. That perfection created war in the heavenly realms. Satan has been trying to destroy us ever since. If Satan is a god of anything, it is jealousy, deceit, and the father of lies. Evolution is a lie not supported by any facts at all, and the author of it pages are pretty clear.

If we ever wondered who man's accuser is, it isn't that hard to figure it out. The pages of the Bible are packed with the truth of GOD's word. Did Satan really think that he could accuse of us of not being perfect, a genetic accident if you will? Has he not been accusing us ever since Eve first took a bite of the forbidden fruit? This is not a supposition or theory, it is the written record of the history of man, the Bible. We have been accused of not being perfect by the enemies of GOD, but how could we argue that we are perfect? If you have any intelligence at all and if you believe in this or not, this is a serious question. Despite what you might think, the GOD of perfection knows you, and the truth is as simple as love and your soul can make you perfect.

Is there anyone left to answer the question? Has it ever been answered? When will the question be answered? It has been answered, and the details are just as amazing as the questions. Man's fall in the garden of Eden left us genetically imperfect, for we were introduced to the lie. We could no longer be with the GOD who created us because we were no longer perfect. But in our fallen state, we could still love, and we still had the capacity for compassion.

While we stood accused of not being perfect, we also stood accused of not obeying GOD. We were tricked by the one doing the accusing, but still, GOD is in His word! Despite our loss of perfection, Satan could not take away from us the one thing that still made us desirable to GOD—the capacity to love, for love is the truth. Anyone who has ever seen a newborn baby in the arms of its mother knows out of all of man's emotions, our ability to love and be loved remained still intact and in the eyes of our GOD, love is perfection.

While some were looking for rocks, others were looking for the truth and found GOD. I wouldn't trade places for all the fossils in the universe. Rocks crumble to sand, but the truth is forever. Evolution was invented in a time before genetics existed. It seemed so simple then, it was obvious to the pagan rock worshippers that man evolved. But now, science has come to a point where we can truly accept the miracle of creation. While geneticist delve into the mystery of junk DNA in our human species, I can assure you at one time that our DNA was full of purpose, and the potential was unlimited. But GOD is in His Word! As it was in the beginning, so shall it be in the end.

Just as in the story of Lot and Sodom and Gomorrah in the Bible, Lot asked GOD, "If there are fifty good men in the city, will you not destroy it?" GOD responded, "If there are fifty good men in the city, I will not destroy it." Lot questioned again, "If there are ten good men in the city, will you not destroy it?" GOD responded, "For the sake of ten good men, I will not destroy the city." Lot finally asked GOD, "If there is just one good man in the city, will you not destroy it?" GOD agreed that for the sake of one good man, he would not destroy the city.

In our carnal minds, we think that GOD's agreement on just one good man and he would not destroy the city was because GOD would do it to save the life of that one good man. But you would be misguided to think so, for if there was just one good man (with love in his heart), that good man could change the hearts and minds of ten men, fifty men, or even an entire city and thus the entire world. So for the sake of just one good man, GOD would never destroy us.

This story illustrates GOD's love for just a single soul, but there is more to this story. This offers us a look into the grandeur of his perfect mind. The object of this story would be repeated in the redemption of mankind, for only one man has laid down his life and picked it up again. Our belief is, he has shown the way and will come again to claim his prize. Will the evolutionists be ready? Will they hold their stone relics high in the air and expect admittance into the kingdom of GOD?

We stand accused, but for the sake of one good man, GOD will redeem us, save us, and again one day, he will be with us again in eternity. While he made us perfect, we were perfect no longer, but for the sake of one good man, perfection is attainable. What man could return to life after his life was lost? GOD's proclamation was just and final, "All men will die." GOD still loved us. How could He not? He made us in His image. We were alas fallen, but we love, which like GOD's love, it is eternally perfect. We look for the truth and like GOD, the truth is perfect. We understand that we are no longer perfect, but we know perfection exist. And now you know. GOD's plan is to save us from the eternal death that awaits us all. How could we find our way back from death? By someone who has been there before and returned, and so the curse has been broken and you have been redeemed. I challenge all evolutionists to read the Bible and its stories, you will find opposition to GOD is useless. Perhaps within its passages, you will find the soul you readily admit you don't have.

Evolution is dying it and will take time; it will not happen overnight but make no mistake, it will die. I suppose as they continue to warp the evolution story, someday it will crack and shatter. Soon, Lucy, still walking on human feet, will be displayed at public museums, and the laughing masses will know what she really is, a joke that wasn't funny now or ever standing there with the human feet she never had.

We know what is right, for it is in our hearts. Do we always choose that which is right? Can we see the real truth and know it? Of course, you can, but only if you know the lie for what it is. The Great Deception! As stated earlier, knowledge is power even if it isn't true because popular opinion dictates what is right these days and in days past also. Popular opinion and the so-called intellectuals, they are now just bullies who tell us what to think in the world of the immoral values that they have found for us. Evolutionists have found their way into public funds via public schools and county museums. Some would question, is evolution the official religion of the United States and Great Britain? You might cringe at this possibility, but for every monument to the Ten Commandants that comes down, another Lucy exhibit goes up, but soon that will be no more.

Ah, this world would be a better place if there were no GOD. That is the atheist message. Evolution is a distraction, a deception and a power mad system dedicated to the proposition all gods are created equal and nonexistent. Let us not forget that, all the while, they become rich for their efforts. Pay at the door! Their message is a pitiful attempt to beg the listening audience to accept the fact man is a creature better off without GOD. And now finally, the gist of it all, evolved Homo sapiens like them just have no further use for a GOD anymore. The insistence of removing religious icons and promoting idolatry is common practice now and gaining ground all the time, but like the lie, soon that will be no more.

After all, with baggage like this hanging around our necks, how could we possibly evolve further? Really! The only thing that evolves is those things manipulated by man and so a truth arises.

Evolution gives man a hand in his own creation, a hand that never was. Evolutionists realize this. The religion of evolution makes you look like a child sucking his thumb, all the while holding his blanket trying to assure the adults in the room everything will be okay! This concept like evolution is totally ridiculous and any useful knowledge lost with the impossibility of evolution.

Your pagan religion, like your theory, is hopelessly flawed. You have missed the end result of the evolutionary experiment completely! The alternate viewpoint has played out and is no longer valid. Time to move on! Man is a creature with a desperate need to believe in something greater than himself, and evolution is not it. Man has found the GOD responsible for his creation and everything else observable, conceivable, and not just here but thought out the entire universe.

Man is driven to find the GOD he lost in the garden of Eden, and now you know the truth! Some men are so desperate. They look too cold dumb rocks for the majesty of creation and that pursuit leads them to another creator, another god, and the greatest lie ever told—evolution! Perhaps some people just didn't get the GOD gene, or perhaps they got it but the gene is just flawed. How else could evolution end up leading to the worship of strange gods? It is all just rocks, fake pictures, and the dirt shoveled out of the way in fossil pits trying to bury GOD with a lie.

Those of you who have made a god of rocks, have your fill. Teach each other how man was created out of creatures that never needed our help in the first place. How our closest living relative has never really changed because he refuses to give up his penis bone. Make up endless stories, print artwork, and feel proud you have proven Satan right at least about you. Be comforted with the fact no truly religious man that believes in GOD would ever harm you for "thou shall not kill." Is the peace and false righteousness reciprocating or do you prefer the company of rocks and dead things? Is it time to confess man's drive, for GOD has found its place even in the evolutionary camp for you to dig and scrape the ground looking for a GOD you can't prove evolution but still you look?

As believers in GOD, we seek to believe because it provides more than an exhibit at the museum, for it is a pathway to life. This is a belief in the truth and, of course, our GOD. It provides for the explanation as to why man seeks perfection, and more importantly, the truth which is perfection itself. You can seek the popular opinion and ignore the GOD coursing through your veins, but it will be at your loss and truly sad. The fire will still be in your heart, but it will burn for a strange god and one that lies. We don't seek power or glory, money or fame. We are satisfied with this simple truth. "There is a GOD" and He lives in our hearts. There is no temple that can contain Him, and the only temple He wants is you.

Can we know the nature of GOD? Can we comprehend the truth and know it? Can you stare into the daylight sun and see it? Truly, this is an example as to the true nature of GOD. The sun exists, but to stare at it will surely cause blindness as we are not equipped with eyes that can comprehend its light, but it does exist and is undeniable. This construct explains to us not everything is explainable, but its truth shines nonetheless. While we cannot see Him, He is there, but we have lost the ability to see for our fall from the garden has left our senses damaged but not our hearts. You cannot see a sunspot with naked eyes, but it exists nonetheless. You can feel His warmth, know His truth, but only with our heart, for even the eyes deceive but never a heart set on the path of love and truth and the inevitable outcome of GOD!

For the evolutionists, it is quid pro quo. GOD has denied me a personal audience and so you pass judgment on GOD not just for yourselves but falsely for everyone else. Guess what, we don't need the help and rock worship, just isn't our style; either is evolution. The Bible brings insights that have an eternal truth and sets us on a path of understanding.

The controversy could easily be over had Moses been wrong. If he had said woman was created first, the genetic slideshow would be over for the believers in GOD. But Moses was right and though you may say Moses had a fifty/fifty chance of being right, the odds against evolution are in the billions. The possibility of any protein soup making all of creation is just silly and an attempt to cheapen the truth. Soup comes from a can, man came from GOD! You have mocked GOD and tried to replace Him with a can of soup. Stop sucking your thumbs and lose the blanket. Evolution is dead, for it comes from roots that were never alive!

Moses was the most intelligent man alive at the time; he was educated in the house of the pharaohs. His education included all the knowledge of the Sumerians. Why would it not? Man destroyers always include the culture of the conquered—Greeks to Romans to British to Americans, etc. Moses handpicked the stories he either liked, or GOD told him they were true. Can anyone quote anything written in the Old Testament said by Moses that isn't scientifically true today? I didn't think so.

Man was created first because GOD needed an XY chromosome so it could be split into an XX, hence woman. Moses told you that we all came from one woman; Moses told you that, and he was right. You should not have sex with relatives; Moses told you that, and he was right. The ancient Hebrews used hygiene rules we still use today for living and eating and everything else. Thanks FDA, thanks EPA, thanks CDC. Nope, thanks Moses and so he was right. Intelligence is relative but even more relative when you consider the words of Moses have never been wrong. Moses is totally honest when he said someone else was responsible for everything on earth. He is bigger than we are and wince has he come? The truth is, brothers and sisters, he isn't from around here. The universe is crammed with the impossible, the understandable, and the questions that are asked are simplistic in their approach, but where did it all come from? GOD! The simplest answer makes its truth shine because the alternative viewpoint says it just happened from a random act of impossibility heaped on the improbable and ended with the ridiculousness of it all.

Moses was like the Bible tells us a product of the house of the pharaohs, just a Jewish kid with a leg up so to speak. Compared to the other masses of people, he was just a lost and confused soul at best. But he was the most educated soul alive at the time. Why would GOD speak to Moses? Moses's education made him someone GOD could talk to and Moses could understand his GOD completely. Although Moses was banished from Egypt, he left under penalty of death if he should ever return. That was before he climbed to a mountaintop and talked to GOD! Moses has been vindicated by science, and Darwin's theory was wrong. Darwin found a lie, and Moses found the truth.

In splicing the XY to an XX in humans was GOD's final masterpiece. For according to the Bible, Eve was his last creation. Every man can appreciate the beauty of our women. But many of us thank the GOD of creation for it. Evolutionists, now you know why we don't buy in. There are just too many holes in your story, and you fill those holes with mystery, innuendo, deceit, fake feet, and colorful artwork. The evolutionary story is like reading the first and last chapter in a book and expecting to know the whole story, but the truth is nothing exist in the middle the secret of the evolutionary story revealed at last.

Evolutionists, there are just too many pages missing, and you attempt to fill those pages with misguided imagination and your personal agenda. You try to punish GOD for hurting your feelings, cast judgment on GOD, and pray to rocks in the hope GOD's judgment isn't reciprocating. You set up implausible arguments, make up all the rules, and cry yourselves to sleep when you find it just doesn't work. Your greatest embarrassment is being found out, but to the majority of people, you already have been found out, and your ability to accept the humiliation is admirable but unnecessary, for you need to only look up to find what you are really looking for.

It is true that woman was GOD's last creation on earth; this being true, then GOD truly outdid Himself. All other creatures pale in comparison! When we think of love, kindness, and devotion, we have our mothers to illustrate for us all of these concepts and this truth, "We are loved." Fathers teach strength; mothers teach love. Without either, we would be a lost and sorry lot. Always know this in the absence of GOD's presence, He gave us parents to watch us to help us and in His absence, we were never forgotten for we thrive at His will and always have.

For strength and love are the only path to the perfection we seek. As fathers teach their children strength and mothers teach their children love, GOD teaches both to us and now you know the truth. The joining of two souls in matrimony brings strength and love to a common joining together; GOD, as the mastermind of that covenant. We are made one flesh, and for us husbands, if we are honest to ourselves, our better half—"our wives." For in GOD, the dividing of men and women when joined together, all is complete and made perfect. When we join together with our wives, we create new children, new life, and of course, new love. If you wonder of the love of GOD, consider this, He has shared that love with His creation eternally and now you know the truth!

We forget that Adam had a choice; he could have refused Eve's forbidden fruit. He could have asked GOD for another woman, but alas he loved this one; bones of his bones, flesh of his flesh. It is the most romantic love story ever told from the creation of man to the end of creation. How could GOD condemn us with instant death? For in love, Adam chose to love the creature created for him. So in that love, GOD's condemnation of us was lessened, because like Adam, GOD created us for himself. Just as GOD created Eve for Adam, all of humanity was created by GOD and for GOD.

Can we imagine GOD's heartbreak at Adam's decision to take the punishment with his wife? But because we are humans listening to the human side of story, we cannot realize GOD's elation over the fact He created a creature that was like Him. "We had the capacity to love." Just as Adam and Eve completed the everlasting bond with man and woman, GOD created an everlasting bond between man and GOD. All of this by the simplest formula there is, GOD is forever and He loves us eternally, and now you know!

GOD, like Adam, could have given up on Eve. He could have tried again later with maybe a slight genetic alteration here or there; He might have produced a better woman. But He didn't because He knew, like himself, we were made with all the perfect love He could put in us. What is perfection? The pursuit of truth is the road to perfection; the pursuit of love is eternal and the GOD of our father lives in us for we need Him desperately. GOD is our strength, our rock, and has provided for our salvation. For there is a way out through GOD, and evolution is a poor excuse for solving anything except what lie will work the best in the future of a history that never was.

Rocks are more than a poor substitution for GOD as they mock the GOD who created them. It is worshipping the creation and not the creator. By the way, no matter what idolatrous cult we are talking about—Ammon/Baal, Zeus, Odin, and the list goes on and on—worshipping the creation not the creator is a common theme in all of them, and especially, it is the foundation of evolution! Sorry, evolutionists, evolution isn't new and like the cults of Baal definitely not improved, as rock worship has a very small niche among the masses today, and soon it will be getting smaller.

GOD truly outdid himself by creating us, for He made us like Himself, perfect. GOD created us so perfect it started war in the heavenly realms. Satan has been trying to destroy us ever since. If he is a god of anything, it is a god of jealousy, deceit, and the father of lies. While some were looking for rocks, others were looking for the truth and found GOD. I wouldn't trade places for all the fossils in the universe. Rocks crumble to sand, but the truth is like GOD and it is forever.

If we are distant from GOD, it is because we don't understand Him. Consider this, children understand Him better than we. A child needs protection, shelter, food, and their lives revolve around that protection and most notably love. They understand this concept because you are their protector. The child understands their parents need for protection also, thus GOD! Evolution was invented in a time before genetics existed. It seemed so simple then, it was obvious to the pagan worshippers that man evolved. But now science has come to a point where we can truly accept the miracle of creation. For like Moses would tell you, "It is all true!"

As we believe in GOD, both Christians and Jews alike, we are not perfect. But perfection does exist. As the Jews have faithfully kept GOD's time clock so we would know what time it is on the biblical timeline. Christians have accepted the sacrifice made at Calvary and have accepted the fact that one good man can change imperfection to perfection. GOD's promise to mankind, "As it was in the beginning, so shall it be in the end." Adam and Eve will again be perfect and so will we that believe.

Ask yourself why was the Hebrew temple destroyed seventy years after the death of the Messiah? It may seem obscure why seventy years after the final sacrifice. This is because every Hebrew child born before the Savior's death was born under the old law. All the Hebrew children born after his death (the Messiah) were born under the new law. GOD does not break his covenant with anything or anyone; He is a GOD of perfection, and no one can claim He is not fair or does not follow His own rules. Those born under the old law were destined to finish their predestine agreement with GOD. Make no mistake, seconds after the death of the last person born under the old law was fulfilled; the Roman General Titus was pounding at the gates of the Old City of Jerusalem in AD 70.

My Jewish brothers and sisters, it is no accident that you have been deprived of your temple sacrifices for almost two thousand years. It was not because Rome wanted your temple burned; it was because GOD found the sacrifice of one good man sufficient and no longer required animal sacrifice under the new law. Just as it is sacrilege to sacrifice an unclean animal, no sacrifice is acceptable under the new law for the final atonement has been made.

No witchcraft by any being ever created can cast a curse on a believer in the true GOD. The greatest curse Satan could come up with was to hang a righteous man on a cross. This being the seal of a curse of the mighty Roman Empire, as it was the most feared death of all time. They attempted to cast this curse, but the curse was broken now and forever. Be free and realize it was for you and like Adam, we breathe the breath of life by his Holy Spirit.

The keys to death, hell, and the grave are held firmly in the hands of he that knows when, where, and how to use them. GOD does not lie. He must keep His word; it is His eternal bond with us. This makes us perfect under the new law and our GOD—a GOD of truth, love, and eternally perfect. Are we to believe that the GOD of perfection would leave the souls of His Hebrew children without forgiveness from AD 70 until now? It would seem that at the last trumpet, we will all know and accept that one good man for who he is—the son of the Living GOD!

My Christian brothers and sisters, do not feel freely vindicated under the new law but apostate under the old law. While you have accepted the savior, you worship GOD on the first day of the week Sunday. This is the day the Lord started his creation, not the day it ended. Shabbat/Saturday is the word in Hebrew for the last day of the week, and now you know. The worship of GOD on Sunday was never changed by any scripture. Even in the New Testament, it was never written that Sunday was the new Shabbat (Sabbath).

Sunday worship defies the sun god Ra. Again, this is to worship the creation (the sun), not the creator GOD. To worship the sun dictates the sun is the deity that made the earth and everything possible, and it is a lie. If you don't believe this, then look into the midnight sky and consider billions of stars calling the sun worshippers liars. There are those who would keep the Sunday worship simply because it's just easier on their schedule. Can we begin to see that we forget GOD's laws because it is easier on us? Imagine having a doctor's appointment on Thursday at eleven o'clock, but you show up at eleven o'clock on Friday. You shouldn't count on being seen, but GOD knows you worship on Sunday is out of ignorance and deception but because He is just and right. Yes, you will be seen.

GOD has a special blessing for those that keep his Shabbat/Saturday worship for the first Christians observed the true Shabbat, and although just a few in number, they evangelized the world under the penalty of death from Rome. The first Christians were burned, stoned, crucified, and fed to wild animals in the arena, but they helped save the world under the new law for they spread his truth even under penalty of death. Although one might relegate man to a simple role of wait and see. In GOD's real church, its members are alive and an active participant in God's real plan for us. As it was in the beginning, so shall it be in the end!

On the subject of some people do what is just easier on them, this extends beyond convenience; it also extends to the profit margin. If they could put aluminum in jet fuel to improve fuel economy, would they do it? After all, the nanoparticles only end up over the population centers of the world. What's a little aluminum between friends? Let's suppose they did something like that, would it cause the sunlight to disperse differently? Would fewer particles of light reflect back into space like they should normally? Would our atmosphere heat up or cool down? Could they blame global warming and convince you that they needed a new tax to solve the problem?

You should know in a country where many people are deficient in magnesium, putting aluminum in your body isn't that good of an idea for anyone. But in a world where there is no place to get rid of things like toxic fluoride, the solution is to convince the population fluoride prevents cavities. Problem solved, fluoride disposed, mouthful by mouthful. The disposal problem goes away overnight, and it did. The communist put fluoride in the water of some subjugated countries; it causes people to be more docile. If you don't think so, look up Prozac. Enough said on this subject until you realize the truth. It's all about the buck.

But they would never let you put toxic substances in your body for control of your mind, would they? Fluoxetine also known as Prozac and also Sarafem has a chemical formula $C_{17}H_{18}F_3NO$, and the F is not for fun. Another ingredient in rat poison is Flocoumafen, an anticoagulant that causes the targeted rats to bleed to death, and its chemical formula is $C_{33}H_{25}F_3O_4$. But speculation is, is it good for your teeth? That's what it says on the front of the box, but on the back of the box, you will find the phone number for the poison control center in considerably smaller writing, of course.

I suppose if someone was so cold as to do a thing like that, they would need to tell you just a little lie. You should consider this, is it the big lies that can harm you? No, it's the little ones; but only if they can get away with the big lies first. Evolution, atheism, and the biggest lie of them all that there is no GOD.

In a world where it would seem some want a new world order, if they had one, would they tell you the truth if they had a truth to tell? Would they tell you they prefer a world without GOD? Would they tell you who, what, and where to worship? Would they tell you that you were born with the majesty of the creator ingrained in your soul? Probably not, it would be so much simpler just not to care about you at all, and especially, not your spouse or your children.

Would they tell you that the plan is underway for a new world order and the deal is almost complete? Would they tell you that all of Europe is on board? Would they tell you that only one country stands in their way? Would they tell you that they have dominion over the whole world except that one standalone country? Would they tell you that the one standalone country must break their covenant with the GOD who blessed its creation before it can be complete? They will eventually get around to that soon enough. What is it that stands in their way only a few simple pieces of paper?

In Congress, July 4, 1776

The unanimous Declaration of the thirteen united States of America, When in the Course of human events, it becomes necessary for one people to dissolve the political bands which have connected them with another, and to assume among the powers of the earth, the separate and equal station to which the Laws of Nature and of Nature's God entitle them, a decent respect to the opinions of mankind requires that they should declare the causes which impel them to the separation. (Source: Declaration of Independence)

We hold these truths to be self-evident, that all men are created equal, that they are endowed by their Creator with certain unalienable Rights that among these are life liberty and the pursuit of happiness. (Source: United States Constitution)

No other country in the history of the world was created at the request of man from his GOD until the fledgling United States of America broke ties with the most powerful empire in the world, England. It appears that GOD accepted that covenant with the inhabitants of the world's first constitutional republic. This country was allowed to flourish by common agreement; under the separation of church and state, it would be a country without a king and under Protestant guidance, it would have a religious system without a pope.

Now you know the real reason why there must be no GOD. Without GOD, there is no Declaration of Independence, no constitution, and certainly, no bill of rights. For this country was created for a purpose—it was man's first attempt to ask for the protection of GOD for their new country. It should be apparent that GOD accepted this covenant with not only our forefathers but with us also. The New World Order won't have a constitution, bill of rights, and will never accept any Declaration of Independence.

Remember this, in a place and time in the not so distant past, every man, woman, and child were considered precious. That was in a day when they let us have a GOD because they dare not take Him away. During the laying of the framework for this country, everyone wisely feared GOD. Now thanks to the great lie. To them, we are just all chimps. Thanks to the god of rocks and those who would hope for a world without any true GOD. If you are gullible enough to believe in evolution, consider how unhappy the chimps will be with no freedom. This will be especially true for the highly evolved evolutionist whose main purpose will be over, and so then will they. For if there were a world with a GOD, He would see what they have done to his world, to His creation, and to His people and would put a stop to it and so soon He will.

The next big lie will be aliens made us. Actually, it is a better story, simply because it is a newer version and has room for an improved storyline. But let's think about this, it is also a lie conceived because the old lie, evolution, doesn't work anymore. I would suppose if the naysayers and evolutionist like the alien story better, then we will hear more about that later. But when looking into the evolutionist/alien theory, remember this, "Anything but GOD!

Do you know where GOD lives, how He feels, what He knows? Listen carefully and know He lives in the hearts of those who believe! Do you think He will not protect us or not allow us to protect ourselves, for He always has done both of these and more. Will He not fulfill every jot and tittle of what GOD has given the prophets to write and do you understand the words therein?

Great Britain, don't you know who you are? Did you think GOD wouldn't fulfill His promises made clear in the Bible? Is the Bible true? Let us consider this and hear the words of Jeremiah 33:17. "For this is what the Lord says: 'David will have a descendant sitting on the throne of Israel forever.'" Ephraim, you are a mighty nation. You have been driven out of every country in Europe until in your quest for GOD. When you asked for a home, He gave a good one! England, Australia, New Zealand, Canada, you are a great people, and this has been a blessing from GOD. Realize this, no greater blessing can be realized until you know exactly who you are, Ephraim.

If you profess to believe, then why can't you see GOD is showing Bible pages in your lives to believe? The world is lining up against you all and now be the brothers he intended you to be. You are a stubborn lot in a world where all of your enemies would relish your demise; you seek to fight with each other, and both Ireland and England should be very disturbed for your action against each other.

GOD hears every man who calls his name with a clean heart. No matter your differences, you are all still brothers. Both Ireland and England are one and know who you are. GOD has declared the end of these things and has told you so. If you claim to believe, then unite for time is short, and the enemies of GOD silently rally against you. Did you leave the European States because it was best for you or did you do it because GOD declared it so? Can you escape who you are? Those of you who are educated can recite the names of your kings and queens until they are lost in antiquity. GOD gave Jeremiah the command to speak it and it has been so.

Ephraim, remember Manasseh your brother also, for his fate is tied to yours. Your enemies see you as the same side of a coin they detest. Did Manasseh take from you that which was his or did you let him take it because GOD had a covenant to seal with Manasseh? GOD's promise to you both will not be forgotten or unfulfilled. Has he not spoken it before your nations were conceived? Trust in GOD and watch as He brings it into the light of truth. Now tell me, United States, do you know who you are? Has GOD not told you as He clearly declared? Manasseh, who has been given the beautiful land, did you not fight for it and shed blood for it, and when will you believe for GOD speaks His word to you both?

Your enemies know who you are. Did you think they will forget or are your great armies just for show? Did you prosper on your own or by what GOD promised to you before you were born? Mighty Manasseh, do your grateful mothers remember to thank GOD for the peace and safety of their children as they sleep? While they have been promised protection, for Manasseh shall possess the gates of their enemies. Has he not provided a pillow of safety where in your heads find rest?

Has GOD not proclaimed, His two candlesticks would be with him in the end. Both the new law and the old together upheld by both Jew and the children of the house of Joseph Ephraim and Manasseh. You will be his; it has been decreed should the world seek to destroy you, He will protect you, but you must ask for that protection. It all has been written and goes on like a play each day getting closer; bow your heads as you pray and be strong in the spirit of Yahshua.

Are the ten tribes lost or did they prosper while away from the rest of the family of GOD? Will GOD bring them home as the evil in this world changes into a magnificent paradise? Together, let's pray that we soon realize what wonder GOD has in store for us all. Did you never know that Manasseh cast the vote that made Israel a nation because the United States was the only nation strong enough to enforce its decision by peace or by force of arms? Have not our Jewish brothers sought refuge in Manasseh and found it? Did not Ephraim (England) take what was yours form the Turks and give it to you? Has not GOD declared that He blesses those that bless the Jews? Only a brother would show such kindness, and I maintain that like brothers, we must live in protection for each other, for the world is weak and seeks our demise.

Did not the Gentiles live in your land until through Ephraim the promise of GOD was attained? It is thought that Israel will stand alone in the end, but why did the Jews name it Israel? And GOD's ten tribes will surely attend in the last days the land GOD has given it to you all. For only in Israel will the temple rise from ashes long cold from a lesson to mankind, and the message is clear—GOD is in control.

Know the peace of GOD, feel it in your hearts, and realize exactly as it was written so shall it be done. Israel, when will you call upon GOD's intervention? Seek His son for He will protect you for there is no better friend, and He knows who your enemies are before they realize it themselves.

Should all of us fear or rest assured in His promise that He will make us secure in His arms and bless us all but not before you all realize who you are, Israel. All of Israel, listen and know this, all of you, all the ten tribes who were blinded by the knowledge of who you are, and the two who were blinded from your savior. Know this, for all men have fallen short of the Glory of GOD. You have performed brilliantly in your blindness and have spread the word of GOD to the masses and every corner of the world. The time of the past is soon to be over, and to proclaim there is no soul is blasphemy of the Holy Spirit. To say you have no soul is a lie, and to say you have been blind to your soul is the truth. Know this that of all the curses of the dragon himself are nothing compared to the curse a man places on himself when he says there is no GOD, and he claims I have no soul. In saying this, you have blasphemed GOD, His Son, the Holy Spirit, and your very own soul.

Israel (both Ephraim and Manasseh), realize this, your ancestors crossed the sea on dry ground to become the mighty nations you are today. What heritage does evolution give you monkey man? Exactly nothing! When you see the lie for what it is, you find the nothingness it provides, for with the splendor and majesty of creation, you are given a false hope in a cold stone god of ignorance.

As for the truth, this should be known. When you hear the truth, you will know it because it stands alone and holds itself high for this simple fact. Nothing else makes sense! Evolution makes no sense! So we should consider the words of Ezekiel and the truth of those words in regards to who are GOD's people. For as GOD has surely proclaimed from the mouth of His living son. So it was in the beginning, so shall it be in the end.

> The hand of the LORD was upon me, and carried me out in the spirit of the LORD, and set me down in the midst of the valley which was full of bones,
>
> And caused me to pass by them round about: and, behold, there were very many in the open valley; and, lo, they were very dry.

And he said unto me, Son of man, can these bones live? And I answered, O Lord GOD, thou knowest.

Again he said unto me, Prophesy upon these bones, and say unto them, O ye dry bones, hear the word of the LORD.

Thus saith the Lord GOD unto these bones; Behold, I will cause breath to enter into you, and ye shall live:

And I will lay sinews upon you, and will bring up flesh upon you, and cover you with skin, and put breath in you, and ye shall live; and ye shall know that I am the LORD.

So I prophesied as I was commanded: and as I prophesied, there was a noise, and behold a shaking, and the bones came together, bone to his bone.

And when I beheld, lo, the sinews and the flesh came up upon them, and the skin covered them above: but there was no breath in them.

Then said he unto me, Prophesy unto the wind, prophesy, son of man, and say to the wind, Thus saith the Lord GOD; Come from the four winds, O breath, and breathe upon these slain, that they may live.

So I prophesied as he commanded me, and the breath came into them, and they lived, and stood up upon their feet, *an exceeding great army.*

Then he said unto me, Son of man, *these bones are the whole house of Israel:* behold, they say, Our bones are dried, and our hope is lost: we are cut off for our parts.

Therefore prophesy and say unto them, Thus saith the Lord GOD; Behold, *O my people*, I will open your graves, and cause you to come up out of your graves, and bring you into the land of *Israel*.

And ye shall know that I am the LORD, when I have opened your graves, *O my people*, and brought you up out of your graves,

And shall put my spirit in you, and ye shall live, and I shall place you in your own land: then shall ye know that I the LORD have spoken it, and performed it, saith the LORD.

The word of the LORD came again unto me, saying,

Moreover, thou son of man, take thee *one stick*, and write upon it, For *Judah*, and for the children of *Israel* his companions: then take *another stick*, and write upon it, For *Joseph*, the stick of *Ephraim* and for all the *house of Israel* his companions:

And join them *one to another into one stick*; and they shall *become one* in thine hand.

And when the children of thy people shall speak unto thee, saying, Wilt thou not shew us what thou meanest by these?

Say unto them, Thus saith the Lord GOD; Behold, I will take the stick of *Joseph*, which is in the hand of *Ephraim*, and *the tribes of Israel* his fellows, and will put them with him, even with the *stick of Judah*, and make them one stick, and they shall be one in *mine hand*.

And the sticks whereon thou writest shall be in thine hand before their eyes.

And say unto them, thus saith the Lord GOD; Behold, I *will take the children of Israel from among the heathen*, whether they be gone, and will gather them on every side, and bring them into their *own land*:

And I will make them one nation in the land, on the mountains of Israel; and one king shall be king over them all; they shall no longer be two nations, nor shall they ever be divided into two kingdoms again.

They shall not defile themselves anymore with their idols, nor with their detestable things, nor with any of their transgressions; but I will deliver them from all their dwelling places in which they have sinned and will cleanse them. Then they shall be my people, and I will be their God.

"David My servant *shall be* king over them, and they shall all have one shepherd; they shall also walk in My judgments and observe My statutes and do them.

Then they shall dwell in the land that I have given to Jacob My servant, where your fathers dwelt; and they shall dwell there, they, their children, and their children's children, forever; and My servant David *shall be* their prince forever.

Moreover, I will make a covenant of peace with them, and it shall be an everlasting covenant with them; I will establish them and multiply them, and I will set My sanctuary in their midst forevermore.

My tabernacle also shall be with them; indeed, I will be their God, and they shall be My people.

The nations also will know that I, the LORD, sanctify Israel, when my sanctuary is in their midst forevermore." (Ezek. 37:1–28; emphasis mine)

When the conversation leads to the question, can you speak to GOD? The answer is more compelling than you would believe.

Some have been listening to GOD since before they were born... Impossible? Did you think, after six thousand years, GOD would not perfect His plan? Some have had dreams so powerful and profound the words to describe the events would boggle the carnal mind. GOD has saved His best for last and now you know who you are! Can you speak to GOD because He is listening? Can GOD speak to you because the roar is deafening once you realize evolution is a contemptible lie?

When I first started writing this book, my wife asked me what it was about? I told her that it was a book about the lie of evolution. She cautioned me that she feared some harm may come to me for some may find me a lunatic or I might be arrested. I reminded my wife that I have a very special Hebrew name. My name is Daniel; its meaning is, "GOD is my Judge." If my writing finds your approval, then you know what time it is on the biblical timeline. GOD's speed and best of an eternal fortune, brothers and sisters. And if you find my writing considerably painful and you find the subject matter condemnable, then consider this, if I find the condemnation of the entire world over this book...My name is Daniel...and GOD is my Judge!

References

"7 Foot Tall Giant Gibbons?" frontiersofzoology.blogspot.com.

"Berra on Darwin." https://www.sciencedaily.com/releases/2010/05/ 100503111420.htm.

"Genetic Variation of Chimp Species." *Science Daily*. April 22, 2007.

"God's Introduction to Moses." Exodus 3:4–6, NKJV.

"Lucy: Did She Walk Like Us?" answersingenesis.org.

"Obsessive-Compulsive Disorder." NAMI: National Alliance on Mental Illness.

"ScientificMethod."http://www.creationstudies.org/Education/isevolu tion science.html.

"T. Rex Soft Tissue Found Preserved." *National Geographic*. https:// news.nationalgeographic.com/news/2005/03/0324_050324_ trexsofttissue.html.

"The Fall of Lucifer." Isaiah 14:12–14, NKJV.

Cann, Rebecca L., Mark Stoneking, and Allan C. Wilson. "Mitochondrial DNA and Human Evolution." *Nature*, 325:31– 36. January 1, 1987.

Constable, Julie L., Mary V. Ashley, Jane Goodall, and Anne E. Pusey. "Noninvasive Paternity Assignment in Gombe Chimpanzees." Wiley Online Library. December 21, 2001.

Darwin, Charles. "Absence of Transitional Forms."

Darwin, Charles. "Argument Against Evolution."

Darwin, Charles. "Breakdown of Evolutionary Theory in Absence of Transitional Forms."

Dawkins, Richard. "Put Your Money on Evolution." *New York Times*, p. 35. April 9, 1999.

Eldredge, Niles. "Tremendous Anatomical Conservation."

Everding, Gary. Washington University in Saint Louis theSource. March 20, 2013.

Ezekiel 37, NKJV.

forerunner.com. "Lucy Fails Test as Missing Link." Article by editorial staff. December 22, 2007.

Fossils, Teeth and Sex: New Perspectives on Human Evolution. University of Washington Press, 1987. (Stern and Sussman write in the American Journal of Physical Anthropology, 60:279–313.

Gibbons, Ann. "Calibrating the Mitochondrial Clock." *Science*, 279:28–29. January 2, 1998.

Gould, Stephen Jay. "Rarity of Transitional Forms."

Hanegraaff, Hank. *The Face That Demonstrates the Farce of Evolution.* Nashville: Word Publishing, 1998.

http://physics.suite101.com/article.cfm/theory vs hypothesis vs law# ixzz0tT5b0Hf5.

https://answersingenesis.org/human-evolution/lucy/lucy-make-over-shouts-a-dangerously-deceptive-message-about-our-supposed-ancestors/.

https://www.nami.org/Learn.../Mental-Health-Conditions/obsessive-compulsive-disord...

Huse, Scott M. *The Collapse of Evolution.* "Nebraska Man," pp. 97–98.

ICA stones. http://pseudoarchaeology.org/b03-ross.html.

Jeremiah 33:17, NLT

Lemonick, Michael. "Everyone's Genealogical Mother." *Time*, p. 66. January 26, 1987.

Leviticus 18:6–16, NKJV.

Lewin, Roger. "The Unmasking of Mitochondrial Eve." *Science*, 238:24–26. October 2, 1987.

Matthew 5:48, NKJV.

Morris, Andrew A. M., and Robert N. Lightowlers. "Can Paternal mtDNA be Inherited?" *The Lancet*, 355:1290–1291. April 15, 2000.

Morris, John D. "Evidence" for human evolution.

Morris, John D. "Was Lucy an Ape Man?" ice.org.

Parsons, Thomas J., et al. "A High Observed Substitution Rate in the Human Mitochondrial DNA Control Region." *Nature Genetics*, 15:363.1987.

Philip, Awadalla, Adam Eyre-Walker, and John Maynard Smith. "Linkage Disequilibrium and Recombination in Hominid Mitochondrial DNA." *Science*, 286:2524–2525. December 24, 1999.

Rodriguez-Trelles, Francisco, Rosa Tarrio, and Francisco J. Ayala. "Erratic Overdispersion of Three molecular Clocks: GPDH, SOD, and XDH." *Proceedings of the National Academy of Sciences*, 98:11405–11410. September 25, 2001.

Rodriguez-Trelles, Francisco, Rosa Tarrio, and Francisco J. Ayala. "A Methodological Bias Toward Overestimation of Molecular Evolutionary Time Scales." *Proceedings of the National Academy of Sciences*, 99:8112–8115. June 11, 2002.

Schwartz, Marianne and John Vissing. "Paternal Inheritance of Mitochondrial DNA." *New England Journal of Medicine*, 347:576–580. August 22, 2002.

seaworld.com (see gorilla physical characteristics).

Strauss, Evelyn. "mtDNA Shows Signs of Paternal Influence." *Science*, 286:2436. December 24, 1999.

Stringer, C.B. and P. Andrews. "Genetic and Fossil Evidence for the Origin of Modern Humans." *Science*, 239:1263–1268. March 11, 1988.

Thomas, Brian. "Lucy's New Foot Bone Is Actually Human." http://www.icr.org/article/lucys-new-foot-bone-actually-human/

Tierney, John, Lynda Wright, and Karen Springen. "The Search for Adam and Eve." *Newsweek*, pp. 46–52. January 11, 1988.

Williams, Sanders. "Another Surprise from the Mitochondrial Genome." *New England Journal of Medicine*, 347:609–611. August 22, 2002.

About the Author

Born in Los Angeles Hospital in 1954, my parents always supported me and made sure I got the best education available at public schools. It was discovered that at the age of fifteen, I was dyslexic and could not read at grade level. The only remedy at the time was a speed-reading course, which broke the bonds of my dyslexia forever. That summer, I read everything I could get my hands on including the Bible, cover to cover, and that changed my life forever. At the age of eighteen, I entered the Marine Corps and witnessed the horrors man unleashed against each other. I have been on a quest for knowledge ever since. I have studied Hinduism and the Buddhism religion and found many truths, but after a lifetime of study, I found the only real truth—GOD and the all-encompassing truth of what He wants for us all, eternal life. If you have heard GOD whisper and wondered if it was real, it was. He wants no temple, for the only temple He wants is you, and now you know.

CPSIA information can be obtained
at www.ICGtesting.com
Printed in the USA
LVHW012335290321
682892LV00011B/442